I0069326

THE INNOVATOR'S METHOD

Bringing New Ideas To Markets

Written by
Melina Padayachy

Cap Innovate

Copyright © 2015 Melina Padayachy

All Rights Reserved

Publisher: Cap Innovate, London

ISBN: 978-0-9564824-2-6

For further details please go to: **www.innovatorsmethod.com**

I would like to dedicate this book to you, the innovators and entrepreneurs, who are brave enough to walk what is often a lonesome and uncertain path, to bring new ideas to markets.

Table of Contents

Acknowledgement

This book has taken me on a journey of learning and discovery, and I would like to thank all those who have directly or indirectly encouraged me in my endeavour.

To begin with, my heartfelt thanks go to the creative team who helped bring this project to execution. More specifically, I would like to thank Dragan Bilic for the beautiful book cover. Few people can capture the essence of one's vision, and Dragan's talent and passion for his craft can be both seen and felt. Then, I would like to thank Stream Design Studio for the creative logo. Last, I would like to express my thanks to Bikash Ranjan Kumar and team Inventace for the design of the website, www.innovatorsmethod.com and Dezven for the design of http://nextcurveglobal.com

I would also like to thank few friends and some of my LinkedIn colleagues, who were kind enough to provide me with some feedback when the book was still in its early stages. My heartfelt thanks go first of all to Mark Golinsky. Mark diligently read through my work, and I am extremely grateful for his help and critical analysis.

I am also extremely grateful to Mike Hatrick from Climate-KIC Nordic, Simon Philbin from Imperial College, Stephen Moss from Greener Moss, Steve Ardire, Advisor to software start-ups, and Prof Daniele Archibugi from Birkbeck University of London, for their feedback on what was then a research paper/"Minimum Viable Book". Their comments shaped my decision as to whether I should turn the research paper into a book.

Then, I would like to thank Barry Calpino, former VP of Breakthrough Innovation for Kraft, and now Adjunct Professor of Marketing at Kellogg School of Management, for his positive comments on the book. Barry confirmed that there was a lack of science behind the discipline of innovation and that more tools and strategies were needed to help innovators. Barry also mentioned that he used the framework to generate new product ideas. Thus, the knowledge that this book fulfils an existing "job to be done" of innovators, gives me an even greater impetus to bring it to market.

Enough of the excitement though and let's talk about the realities of doing research. Whilst the prospect of discovering interesting insights is the light that keeps an inquisitive mind going, the journey can be an uncertain one. In that respect, I would like to thank my friends and family for their encouraging words when the journey became challenging.

First, my gratitude goes to all my friends, more specifically to my dearest Melina, Dana, Nasreen, Branthi, Cecile, Pam, Jess, Yo, Nan, Alan, Soraya, Susan and Paul, Andrew, Paul, Fred, Georges, Melanie, Sunil and Fiona. Their encouraging words meant a lot to me.

I am grateful to my family as well, for being here. My thanks go to my mum, Sarojah, and my siblings and siblings in law, Jenny, Kevin, Storm and Kajal, for being an important part of my life. I am also thankful to my dearest Grandma, uncles, aunts and cousins, for reminding me of what's important.

Then, I would like to express my heartfelt thanks to Steven Noel Rungasamy. Without Steven's encouragement, this book would undoubtedly not have seen the light of day. Steven also read though the drafts of the book and I am really grateful for his feedback.

Last but not least, I am grateful to my dad, Siva, and my mum, Sarojah, for being my inspiration.

Preface

Finding ideas that markets would love can often seem like a feat that only few people are lucky enough to achieve. Study the stories of Amazon, Google and Starbucks for instance, and you would find that in each case, the innovators almost stumbled upon their ideas by chance.

Indeed, prior to the genesis of Google, Larry Page was a student at Stanford University and he was aspiring to download the internet on his computer and rank web pages based on their popularity. As a result, Google's proprietary Page Ranking technology was born, making Google the leading search engine in the world. For Amazon, Jeff Bezos came across an important piece of information about the exponential rise of the internet while researching opportunities for his boss and as a consequence, he created what is now the leading online bookstore in the world. Next, the idea to sell espresso in a coffee bar popped into Howard Shultz's mind while he was attending a conference in Milan and he saw espresso bars at nearly every road corner. As a result, he wanted to import the concept to the United States and today, Starbucks is one of the leading coffee places in the world.

In all three cases, it would seem that the innovators were either in the right place at the right time or they were trying to solve the right problem. As a result, one may be tempted to conclude that innovation is essentially serendipitous and that any attempt to decode it would be futile.

Yet, if you examine how past innovations impacted their markets, you would find certain distinctive patterns that could be emulated. For instance, some innovations capitalised on *existing trends* while others were caused by *growing and changing trends*, and still others, *created new trends*. Of even more significance, are the facts that past innovators were aware of the market impact of their ideas and they adopted concomitant development, go-to-market and scaling strategies.

The implications are quite significant because often, new ideas are subsumed under the generic banner of innovation and no distinction is made among their market impacts. As a result, some often fail to take off. Indeed, scroll through the post-mortems of failed ideas[1] and you would see that often, ideas failed because their market impact was wrongly framed.

Thus, focusing on the market impact of past innovations, this book will identify *three axes* along which the organisation can innovate and *nine strategies of looking for ideas*. It will also show you that you do not have to dive into an innovation venture, armed with your gut feeling and your right brain only.

This brings us to the question: *Is this book for you?*

If you are an entrepreneur or if you work in an organisation that is pursuing an innovation strategy, this book will provide you with the strategies for sourcing, developing, commercialising and scaling different types of ideas. Also, if you are an investor, an understanding of the market impact of ideas could inform your decision about whether to invest or not in an idea, and it would give you a better gauge of the expected rate of return on different types of ideas.

Thus, in chapter *one*, the nine strategies of looking for ideas will be outlined. Chapter *two* will show you how to evaluate the market impact of your ideas. Chapter *three* will show how different ideas would need different development strategies. Chapter *four* will expound on the different commercialisation and scaling strategies that different ideas would need, and chapter *five* will examine how ideas failed because innovators did not properly frame the market impact of their ideas and as a result, they applied the wrong development, go-to-market and scaling strategies.

You may be wondering how this book differs from other entrepreneurship and innovation books. The basic proposition of this book is that it identifies a *missing link* or rather, a factor that is often overlooked in the process of bringing new ideas to market, and that is, *the evaluation of the market impact of an idea*. It also posits that the market impact of an idea would play a crucial role in the process of bringing new ideas to market, because the market impact of an idea would affect its development, go-to-market and scaling strategies.

Hopefully, the case studies described in this book will successfully guide you through the strategies that you would need to bring different types of ideas to market.

If you have any questions/ comments, please feel free to send me an email at **melina@innovatorsmethod.com**

THE INNOVATOR'S METHOD

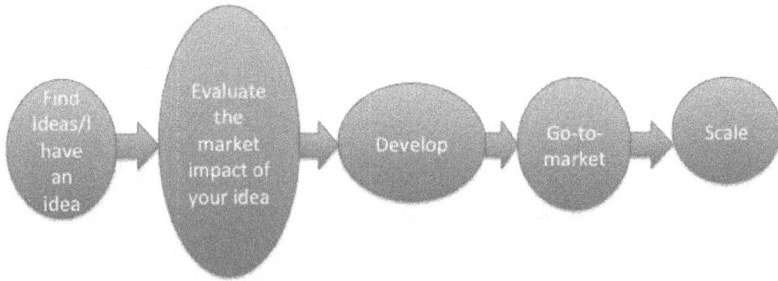

Introduction

I will start this book in a perhaps unconventional way, by introducing two ideas that did not take off or rather, that did not take off as quickly as expected. Dinnr was a start-up founded in July 2012 by Michal Bohanes, a young entrepreneur. While working at Google, Bohanes was quite frustrated about his meals. Not an inventive cook himself, his dinner options consisted of cooking from scratch, ordering a take away or going to a restaurant.[1] Although he wanted to cook more, Bohanes thought that it would be too time consuming to get a recipe book, go though it, select a recipe, go out to get the ingredients and start cooking.[2]

Thus emerged the idea for Dinnr. Dinnr was targeted at young urban professionals, i.e young couples and young families, who would want to introduce variety in their cooking, and it offered recipes online which markets could select and Dinnr would send them all the ingredients in the right amounts, along with the step by step cooking instructions.

The idea was most certainly full of promise. Yet, after nearly two years, the company had to close down because it had only 220 customers and it did not have enough traction to be profitable.

In a similar vein, Flowtab was a start-up founded by two entrepreneurs, Kyle Hill and Mark Townsend, in March 2011. Conceived one night at 2am, the idea aimed at streamlining the drink ordering process in bars via an app that customers could download on their phone and the orders would be received on iPads that were connected to the tills in bars.[3] The idea seemed to be solving the *"trading floor syndrome"*[4] that bar counters would usually experience, i.e of customers flocking around the counter, shouting their orders and waving their money in a desperate attempt to be heard. Yet again, after two years, the founders decided to cease the start-up's operations because the company had only 12 regular users across 9 bars.[5]

Those two stories are far from being unique. Indeed, a study showed that 42% of 101 start-ups attributed their failure to a lack of market fit.[6]

Question is: *Could those start-ups have done anything differently to achieve better market fit and increased adoption?*

The following chapters will seek to answer this question.

FIND IDEAS

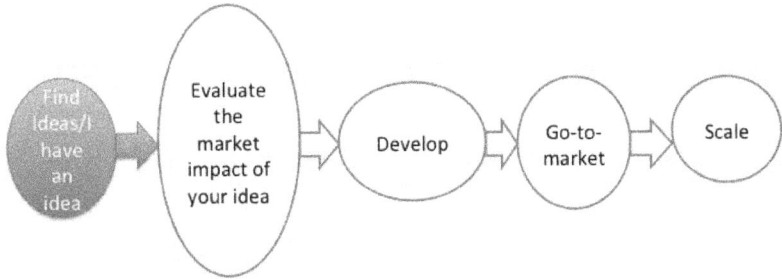

1. Find ideas

1.1 Strategies for finding ideas

<u>Key Points:</u>
The three axes of innovation:
1) Look for ideas within existing trends.
2) Look for ideas within growing and changing trends.
3) Create new trends.

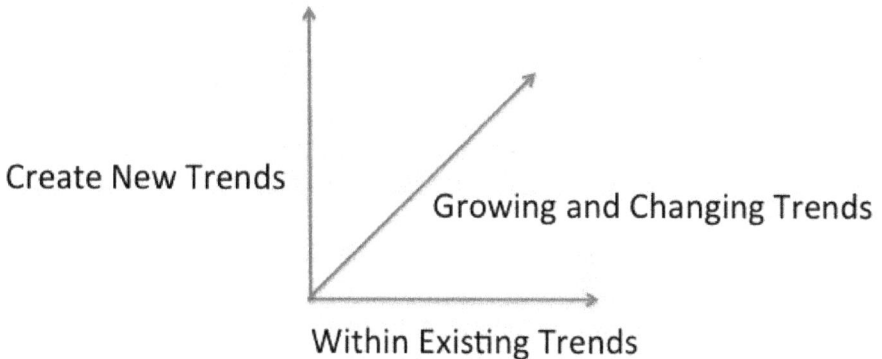

Create New Trends

Growing and Changing Trends

Within Existing Trends

Perhaps one of the most crucial questions facing start-ups and businesses pursuing an innovation strategy is the following:

How does one find ideas that markets will find compelling?

Stories of successful innovations such as the iPhone and the iPod often make businesses marvel at Apple's seeming prescience. However, do innovations owe their successes to serendipitous moments of inspiration or can they occur through conscious design?

Job to be done
Among the various strategies for finding ideas, which have emerged in the past decades, the *"job to be done"* concept[1] is perhaps one of the most compelling. The job to be done concept is a strategy that

involves identifying the jobs that markets would seek to get done by hiring particular solutions. As Clayton Christensen explains in the *Innovator's Solution*, markets *"hire"* solutions to satisfy specific jobs to be done. For example, a dad buying milkshake for his child in the afternoon would be trying to satisfy the job of being a good parent while in the morning, the same milkshake would satisfy the job of making his car journey to work less boring.[2] Thus, by looking at existing solutions that markets would *"hire"*, innovators could try to understand the jobs that markets would seek to get done, and they could then tailor their solutions to more adequately suit the needs of markets. For instance, the afternoon milkshake could be made thinner to reduce the amount of time that children would spend drinking it, while in the morning, it could be made thicker, with pieces of fruits in it, to render the car journey less boring.[3]

Solution -> Morning milkshake
Job to be done = Make journey to work less boring

Solution -> Afternoon milkshake
Job to be done = Be a good parent

Yet, while an analysis of the job to be done provides a basis for identifying existing market needs, it would be less adequate for finding ideas that would create new needs. For instance, it would have been difficult for Howard Schultz to come up with the idea for Starbucks by looking at the jobs that markets were trying to get done, because markets didn't yet know that they would enjoy the romance of drinking coffee in a café. As Howard Schultz recounts, *"people didn't know they needed a safe comfortable neighbourhood gathering place. They didn't know they would like Italian espresso drinks. But when we gave it to them, the fervour of their response overwhelmed us."*[4] Thus, identifying the job to be done would not be useful when trying to find ideas that would create new needs.

Here, it may be worth noting that prior to the creation of Starbucks café, people drank coffee for perhaps various reasons, i.e coffee fulfilled different jobs to be done. In some cases, people probably drank coffee for a caffeine shot in the morning. In other cases, perhaps they drank coffee to simply have a break. However, *enjoying the romance of Italian coffee* in a safe neighbourhood place was not a job that the American market was trying to get done. Starbucks successfully created a new job to be done for the American market.

Incidentally, if you consider different ideas that have been successfully commercialised in the past, you would find that they impacted their respective markets differently.

First axis for innovation: Within existing trends

Find:
----Idea that improves on existing jobs to be done based on pain points experienced by markets.
----Idea that improves on existing jobs to be done based on your subjective perception.
----Idea that improves on existing jobs to be done but changes the habits of markets.

Consider Google for instance. In 1996, internet surfers were struggling with one problem: *How to make sense of all the information on the web.* At the time, Sergey Brin and Larry Page were PhD students at Stanford University and like most web surfers, they used search engines to sift through the vast amount of information on the web. However, most search engines fell short. As Rajeev Motwani, Brin's advisor at the time, recalled, a new search engine called Inktomi had been developed at Berkeley and when Motwani typed Inktomi in Inktomi's search box, to his surprise, nothing came up. Inktomi could not find itself.[5] Brin and Motwani were convinced that there had to be a better way of searching the web. During that time, Page *"began hunting around the web using a new search engine called Alta Vista."*[6] There, he discovered something interesting. Unlike other search engines, Alta Vista also displayed *"obscure information about something called links."*[7] Intrigued, Page wondered what could be learned from analysing the links.

Two important findings emerged. The first one was that the number of links that pointed to a page would determine the popularity of the web page. The second one was that not all links were created equal and so, Page assigned different weights to different links.[8] Soon enough, Brin and Page, together with their respective advisors, came up with a mathematical formula that could rank web pages based on their popularity. They named their technology Page Rank and the latter became the technology behind Google's search engine.

What distinguished Google's search engine was the fact that it improved on an existing job to be done of searching for information on the web. Alta Vista was the best search engine at the time and although "*it did a reasonably good job of canvassing the internet, it did a poor job of ranking search results.*"[2] Through its game changing technology, Google provided a better search engine that allowed it to become the leading search engine provider in the world.

Existing job to be done = Finding information on the web.

Solutions: Search engines -> Page ranking search engine (Google)

So, one strategy of looking for ideas would be to look for game changing solutions to existing jobs that need to be done. Solutions would be game changing if they markedly improve on existing solutions and redefine prevailing standards.

Likewise, if you examine how the iPod impacted markets, you would find that it improved on the existing job to be done of listening to music on the go. Presumably, the iPod fulfilled several jobs to be done (such as the "job" of looking trendy or the "job" of feeling part of the Apple community, etc), but one of them, was to listen to music on the go. The job to be done of listening to music on the go was being carried out by mp3 players and the iPod took over the mp3 market via its game changing design that improved upon the user experience.

However, the need for a better mp3 player was not gauged from the pain points experienced by markets. Rather, it was based on the subjective perception of Steve Jobs. Jobs thought that existing mp3 players at the time "*offered a lacklustre experience, and everyone at Apple agreed.*"[10] Mp3 players did not have much storage capacity either and they were massive. Apple came up with a product that improved on the overall experience of users. But since the improvement was based on the subjective perception of the Apple team, the latter had to actively promote the value offered by the iPod.

Existing job to be done = Listening to music on the go

Solutions: Walkman -> CD player -> Mp3 Player -> iPod

Similarly, LinkedIn did not look at the pain points experienced by professionals when it launched. Rather, Reid Hoffman and his co-founders thought that the widespread use of the internet could improve on the job to be done of networking for professionals. The improvement was based on the subjective perception of the innovators. As a result, LinkedIn had to educate markets about the value of using the solution. They also hired a PR agency after six months to generate awareness about the value of the solution. [11]

Existing job to be done: Professional networking

Solutions: Face to face -> Online professional network (LinkedIn)

Therefore, a different way of looking for ideas would be to subjectively imagine how existing jobs to be done could be improved, especially when compared to existing solutions.

Now, take a look at how Salesforce.com's Software as A Service (SaaS) impacted its market. Salesforce.com was launched by Marc Benioff in 1999 and it revolutionised the way that software was sold. The idea for Salesforce.com had been "simmering" when Benioff was still a Senior Vice President at Oracle. Benioff had been at Oracle for ten years and he had, to his dismay, become what he described as a *"corporate lifer"*.[12] That was when he decided to take a sabbatical from work and rented a hut in Hawaii in an attempt to rethink his life. Mulling one day over how the internet and websites such as Amazon.com were changing the way that customers shopped, he surmised: *Why couldn't the internet change the way that business customers shopped?*[13] Being fully aware of the inefficiencies and complexities associated with the use and installation of traditional CRM (customer relationship management) enterprise software, Marc saw the potential of an online CRM software, i.e a CRM software that would be purchased, delivered and operated online. And thus was born Salesforce.com.

Salesforce.com's vision was to make software easy to use and to install.[14] Its aim was to improve on an existing job that was being done, i.e customer relationship management. The challenge facing Benioff, however, was that the new business model entailed a change in the habits of markets, i.e it offered a new way of carrying out an existing job to be done. Therefore, its market impact was quite different to the market impact of Google's search engine because the latter did not change the habits of markets.

Existing job to be done = Managing customer relationship

Solutions: Enterprise software -> Online CRM software (changed habits of markets)

In a similar vein, Johnathan Abrams's idea for Friendster changed the way that an existing job was being done, i.e it changed the way that friends communicated. When Abrams left Netscape in 1998, he started toying with a new idea: *"A software that could integrate one's online and offline identities."*[15] At the time, online dating was becoming an established trend and one morning, while walking with his friend in Santa Clara Park, Abrams had the idea of a website where *"each person would have a standardised homepage, à la Match.com (the online dating website). But instead of simply advertising their interests and good looks, users could link their profiles to those of their friends, creating a network of connections that would mirror those that existed in the real world."*[16] Friendster was launched in March 2003 and by June, it had 835000 members.[17] Friendster improved on and changed the way that friends could communicate with each other, and it spawned a trend in social media.

Technology pushes the frontier of what is possible and it can often improve on the jobs that markets try to get done. A different way of looking for ideas would be to consider how newly established technologies or trends could improve on existing jobs to be done or could change the way that the latter are performed.

Existing jobs to be done = Communicating and staying in touch with friends

Solutions: Face to face -> Online social networking sites (changed habits of markets)

Therefore, when innovating within existing trends, your first step would be to look at the jobs that markets would try to get done with existing solutions. An opportunity for innovation would be to consider how existing solutions would fall short of the existing jobs to be done. Another one would be to subjectively imagine how existing jobs to be done could be improved. A third option would be to consider how existing technologies or trends could improve on existing jobs to be done or could change the way that the latter are performed.

Innovating in the bicycle market.

Let's say for instance, that you decide to innovate in the bicycle market. Your first step would be to look at the reasons why markets would travel on bikes. If you find out that some of the jobs that markets would seek to get done by travelling on bicycles are 1) to get to work on time and 2) to exercise and keep fit, you should find out how the bicycle would fall short of the existing jobs to be done.

Solution: Bicycle
Jobs to be done = Get to work on time and exercise and keep fit.

Let's say that your research shows that one of the pain points of using the bicycle is that it is difficult to cycle on rainy days, you could innovate by perhaps offering a bicycle that would incorporate a domed rooftop. There are two caveats that you should however heed.

The first one is: *Would the difficulty of cycling on a rainy day be a pain point that would be big enough that markets would pay to eliminate it?*

And the second one is: *Would markets value the solution, i.e the domed rooftop that you propose?* Indeed, while markets may want to pay to eliminate the pain point of cycling on a rainy day, they may not necessarily like the domed rooftop as a solution. While markets would value the improvement to their existing job to be done, they would not value what you offer.

Let's now say that instead of looking at pain points experienced by markets, you *subjectively* consider that the jobs to be done of getting to work on time and of exercising could be improved with a monitor that shows information about your speed and the distance and time left to reach your destination as well as the amount of calories that you've burnt. The question that you would face is: *Would markets value the improvement to the job to be done?* Sometimes you may think that a job to be done must be improved but in reality, customers would not impart the same amount of value to the improvement.

So, the next step would be to find out how markets would value the improvement to the job to be done that you propose. How markets value your improvement would translate into their willingness to pay for the solution, assuming that the price that you charge is within their reach.

For instance, as mentioned before, Flowtab was a start-up that offered a solution that facilitated the way that drinks were ordered and paid for in bars. Bar customers could order their drinks on their smartphones using the Flowtab app and the bartender would receive the orders on an iPad that was connected to the till. Customers only had to collect their drinks at the bar. While Flowtab improved on the jobs to be done of ordering and paying for drinks, the improvement was based on the subjective perception of the Flowtab founders. Customers were not asking for an improvement in the way they ordered and paid for drinks in bars and although Flowtab's solution improved on the ordering and payment processes, they could not convince markets to pay for the improvement. Here, it could be argued that Flowtab could have found a different way of extracting value from its idea. As Mike Townsend, the founder, acknowledged afterwards, perhaps if he had built enough usage for free and then charged drinks companies for ads, maybe the idea would have succeeded.[18] However, that's an assumption that would still need testing.

The point here, is that your improvement to an existing job to be done should be valued by markets, to the extent that they would use it and you would manage to extract value from the idea. For example, Google's search engine was free to users but because of the great number of users using the search engine, Google could charge advertisers for ads displayed on its search pages.

An equally important point to consider when innovating within existing trends would pertain to whether your solution changes the habits of markets. If it does, its market impact in terms of adoption would be different to the impact of a solution that does not change the habits of markets. If for instance, you came up with a solution that allowed cyclists to have a maximum workout by riding their bicycles without holding the handles. Let's say that the handles could steer automatically. While markets might be happy to adopt the improvement to the job to be done of exercising, they might not be happy to change their habits. Therefore, you would need to test the willingness of markets to change their habits.

Those uncertainties will be addressed in Chapter 3.

Now, the second axis along which the organisation can innovate is within growing and changing trends.

Second axis for innovation: Growing and changing trends

----*Create new jobs to be done.*
----*Change the way that existing jobs are done.*

Growing and changing trends can either render existing solutions obsolete by changing the way that existing jobs are done or they can create the need for new solutions by creating new jobs to be done.

Case in point, in 1982, the internet had created a new trend in the lives of people. By 1994, it was a **growing trend** and as businesses started having a web page and a web address, websites started to proliferate. However, in order to access those sites, users needed an internet browser. Whilst there were few browsers out there, *"the browsers themselves were not easy to get"*, i.e they were not easy to understand and were not *"readily accessible to the average Joe."*[19]

At the time, Marc Andreessen was an undergraduate working at the University of Illinois National Centre for Supercomputing Applications (NCSA) and he decided to *"write a browser that everybody could easily use."*[20] Together with his friend Eric Bina, they wrote up the codes for the first Mosaic browser, which could be downloaded for free on the NCSA website. When Marc graduated in 1993, he was approached by Jim Clark, a Silicon Valley entrepreneur, who was looking for the Next Big Thing. Together, they founded Netscape that commercialised the first user-friendly browser. The internet was creating a new trend and it created a new job to be done for those using it, i.e the need to access websites. Marc Andreessen capitalised on the new job to be done and he created an easy to use browser. Within four months of the launch of Navigator, *"75 percent of the people on the Net were using a Netscape browser."*[21] The widespread use of the internet had created the need for a new solution; the browser.

Growing trend: Internet
New job to be done = Accessing websites

Solutions: Internet browsers -> User-friendly internet browser (Netscape browser)

If you now examine how Amazon came into being, you would find that **growing trends** can also change the way that markets would satisfy existing jobs to be done. In 1994, when Jeff Bezos was tasked with the mission of identifying internet opportunities, he discovered two interesting facts:

1) The internet was growing at the rate of 2300% per year.
2) Books were the most sold items online.[22]

The internet was starting to change the way that an existing job was being done, i.e book purchasing. Bezos was a senior Vice president at DE Shaw (a hedge fund) at the time, and he recommended that the company's first internet play should be selling books, but to his surprise, the idea was rejected.[23] Bezos then decided to resign from the company and *"do this crazy thing-start his own internet bookselling company."*[24] His boss tried to talk him out of the idea and suggested they went for a walk in the park. However, after using his *"regret minimisation framework"*[25] which is a framework that he uses to diminish the number of decisions that he would eventually regret, Bezos knew that, whilst he was sure that he would not regret walking away from his Wall Street bonus, he would regret not participating *"in this thing called the internet."*[26] So, Bezos and his wife Mackenzie left their flat in Manhattan and headed to Seattle to found the online retail company.

At the time, few websites, namely clbooks.com and books.com, had started selling books by email. However, Amazon *"felt that the other companies selling books online were, in their opinion not doing it very well."*[27] The company differentiated itself from the nascent online providers and provided a service that was different and unique. Amazon.com was launched on 16th July 1995. The number of customers reached 23 m and by the end of 2000, it was the 93rd biggest retailer in the US according to the National Retail Federation.[28] A different way of looking for ideas would be to consider how a growing trend could improve on the way that an existing job is being done or could change the way that the latter is performed.

Growing trend: Internet
Existing job to be done = Book purchasing

Solutions: Bricks and mortar book retailer -> Online book retailer (changed habits of markets)

In the same line, it would be important to examine how **changing trends** create *new jobs to be done* or *change the way that existing jobs are done*. For instance, Force.com was launched by Salesforce.com in 2007 and provides a Platform as a Service (PaaS) to help markets create and host their enterprise applications online. It may be worth remembering that Salesforce.com had changed the way that businesses bought and used software and that **change in trend** had created a new job to be done, i.e the need for an online platform that would cater to an increase in demand for different types of applications and would allow customers to create their own software online. As a matter of fact, when Salesforce.com had a critical mass of end users, Benioff saw Platform as a Service as *"the natural extension to SaaS."*[29] As Benioff stated, Salesforce.com could not have started as a platform because they needed the *"critical mass of end users, the hundreds of thousands of customers using the application and providing input so that they could see what markets were looking for and know how to build additional functionality that suited them."*[30] According to a Gartner report, PaaS spending will reach \$2.9 billion in 2016.[31] Therefore, companies should be on the lookout for changes in market trends and identify the new jobs that would be created by changing trends.

Changing trend: Online Software as a service
New job to be done = Hosting online software

Solution -> Online platform as a service

Changing trends can also render existing solutions obsolete by changing the way that existing jobs are done. For example, in 1906, W. K Kellogg realised that an existing job to be done was being carried out in a different way when *"american eating habits began shifting from heavy fat laden breakfasts to lighter grain based meals."*[32] At the time, there were already few cereal companies in Battle Creek, Michigan. W.K discovered that a better flake could be produced using only the corn grit.[33] With its game-shaping product, Kellogg capitalised on the changing market habit (i.e a shift to a healthier diet) and on the existing job that was starting to be done differently (i.e eating breakfast) and it became a leading player in the breakfast cereal market. Thus, innovators should be on the lookout for changes in market habits and they should consider how those shifts would affect or are affecting existing jobs to be done.

Changing trend: Shift to a healthier lifestyle
Existing job to be done = Eating breakfast

Solutions: Fat laden breakfast -> Light grain cereal

Therefore, as an innovator, you should consider how growing and changing trends:
1) Create new jobs to be done.
2) Could improve on and change the way that existing jobs are being done.

A caveat that should however be heeded is that the growth or change in trend must be ascertained, i.e there must be some form of market intelligence or data that would indicate the rate at which the respective trends are growing or changing.

For instance, Boo.com was an online fashion company that was founded in 1998 by two entrepreneurs, Ernst Malstom and Kajsa Leander. Aspiring to be the *"premier online location where the cool and the chic would be able to buy their clothes,"*[34] Boo.com launched with 400 employees in eight offices. However, considering that only 20% of UK households had access to the internet, the company had few visitors to its sites and not enough sales to sustain itself. Furthermore, the website's features could not be fully accessed with the dial up connection in UK households.[35] As a result, the company had to close down two years later. Had Boo.com had the data about the penetration of the internet in the UK, they could probably have been more realistic about the rate of growth of their company. Therefore, when innovating within growing and changing trends, it would be important that you have an idea about the rate of change or the rate of growth of the respective trends.

Now, a perhaps more challenging way of finding ideas would be to follow the Belvita biscuit example.

Third axis for innovation: Create new trends

----Create new jobs that markets may want to get done.

Few years ago, Mondelez international anticipated a new job that breakfast skippers might have wanted to get done, i.e have breakfast. As a result, the company launched Belvita breakfast biscuit in the UK. It was a bet considering that unlike other European people, British people do not usually eat biscuits for breakfast.[36] However, according to *Ingredients Nework.Com Insights*, Belvita's brand sales reached GBP 50m per year by the end of 2012.[37] Clearly, the bet paid off.

Job that breakfast skippers might have wanted to get done = Have breakfast

Solution -> Breakfast biscuits

Likewise, Howard Schultz anticipated a job that the American market might have wanted to get done when he launched the coffee bar in the USA. Schultz's encounter with espresso bars was quite epic and it created a whole new trend. Indeed, in 1983, Howard Schultz had been working at Starbucks for a year when he was sent to Milan to attend an international housewares show.[38] The morning after he arrived, he decided to walk to the trade show that was only fifteen minutes away from his hotel.

As soon as he started his walk, he noticed an espresso bar. He stepped in and was greeted cheerfully by a tall thin man. Standing close to each other at the bar were three customers who were waiting to be served. One of them was served an espresso and the other one was served a cappuccino. And soon it was Schultz's turn and he asked for an espresso. A *"sensual flavour"* crossed his tongue as he took a sip of his first espresso.[39] Half a block later, he saw another espresso bar where a gray haired man behind the counter was greeting each customer by name. They were laughing and talking amicably. Later, Schultz saw few more espresso bars and he was fascinated by the camaraderie among the barristas and the customers.

On that day, Schultz discovered what would become the new mission of Starbucks: *"Selling the ritual and romance of coffee bars."*[40] At that point, he realised that they had to *"unlock the romance and mystery of coffee firsthand in coffee bars."*[41] As he explained, *"the Italians understood the personal relationship that people could have to coffee, its social aspect."*[42] He couldn't believe that Starbucks was in the coffee business, yet was overlooking such a central element.[43]

When Starbucks opened its sixth store at the corner of Fourth and Spring in downtown Seattle in April of 1984,[44] Schultz was given a small corner to test his idea. *"By closing time, about 400 customers had passed through the door-a much higher tally than the average count of 250 in Starbucks' best performing stores."*[45] Within two months, the store was serving 800 customers a day.[46]

It would be worth noting here that prior to the creation of Starbucks café, markets were not trying to enjoy the romance of espresso in a café. Howard Schultz imagined a job that the American people might have wanted to get done and the market adopted the new job to be done. Back then, the Specialty Coffee Association of America predicted that the number of coffee cafés, including espresso bars and carts would rise from 500 in 1992 to 10000 by 1999.[47] Overall, the US Gourmet Coffee market had risen by 18 percent a year from $ 270 million in 1984 to $ 750 million in 1991. Starbucks had successfully created a new trend.[48]

Job that the US market might have wanted to get done = Enjoy the romance of espresso in a safe neighbourhood place

Solution -> Coffee bar

The Belvita and Starbucks examples show that the third axis along which the organisation can innovate is by creating new trends.

The creation of new trends involves the creation of new jobs that markets may want to get done, i.e it involves creating new value propositions that markets may not necessarily need or want to adopt. Trend creating ideas would have a different market impact to ideas that would cater to existing jobs to be done, because the former would sell a new need as opposed to satisfying an existing need. The implication of the market impact of the different ideas will be further discussed in the following chapters.

If we summarise the main different strategies of looking for ideas, we would find that they could happen along the following three axes.

A. Within existing trends:
Within existing trends, markets would hire existing solutions to satisfy existing jobs to be done.
Therefore you could:
1) Identify how existing solutions would fall short of existing jobs to be done and develop or find superior game changing solutions. (E.g game changing technology - Google)
2) Subjectively imagine how an existing job could be improved. (E.g iPod, LinkedIn, Flowtab.)
3) Identify established trends across industries (e.g use of the

internet, use of smartphones, etc) and see how they could be used to markedly improve on existing jobs to be done or change the way that the latter are performed. (E.g Salesforce.com SaaS changed the way that software was bought and used.)

B. Within growing and changing trends:

Growing and changing trends can change the markets' needs for existing solutions by changing the way that existing jobs are done, and they can create the need for new solutions, by creating new jobs to be done.

Therefore, you could:

1) Identify how changing market trends would create new jobs to be done and thus, would create the need for new solutions. (E.g New job to be done of online hosting, created by Software as a Service.)

2) Identify how growing trends would create new jobs to be done and thus, would create the need for new solutions. (E.g The growing use of the microcomputer created the need for IT services. As a result, in 1989, two years after the launch of the microcomputer, Citrix systems developed solutions that enabled IT services.)

3) Identify how growing technologies and growing trends could improve on and change the way that existing jobs are carried out. (E.g The advent of the internet changed the way that books were purchased.)

4) Identify how changing trends/market habits could change the way that existing jobs are done. (E.g Adoption of a healthier diet caused a shift from fat laden breakfast to light grain cereals.)

C. Create new trends:

The creation of new trends involves the creation of completely new habits and new needs of which markets were not aware.

In order to create new trends, you could:

1) Identify the jobs that specific markets may want to get done. (E.g Mondelez International targeting breakfast skippers.)

2) Identify the jobs that markets in general may want to get done. (E.g Starbucks.)

This brings us to the second important question:
How would you source different types of ideas?

1.2. Strategies for sourcing new ideas

A. Within existing trends:
Understand your market.
Take a look at how Google and Salesforce.com came into being and you would find that when examining the jobs that markets would seek to get done, closeness to the users would be necessary. For instance, the Google founders were heavy users of search engines. They were thus in a position to understand the needs of users and the inadequacies of existing solutions. Likewise, Marc Benioff from Salesforce.com had worked in the software industry for years and he thoroughly understood the jobs that software users were trying to get done. He understood that enterprise software was cumbersome to users and his vision was *"to make software easier to purchase, simpler to use and more democratic without the complexities of installation, maintenance and constant upgrades."*[49] Marc also interviewed his former colleagues working in other companies to know what markets did not like.

In contrast, when Ratan Tata, the former chairman of Tata Industries, observed a family of four being transported on a scooter, he made some flawed assumptions about how the job that the market was trying to get done, could be improved. Tata thought that an affordable car would eliminate the danger associated with scooter travel. However, the need for an improvement to the job to be done of transporting middle class families, was purely subjective. Tata never tried to gauge whether the danger of transporting a family on a scooter, was a pain point that markets wanted to eliminate. The Nano also changed the habits of markets and Tata did not investigate what it would take for markets to change their habits.

Existing job to be done: Transport for middle class family
Solutions: Scooter -> Nano (changed the habits of markets)

According to Dain Dunston, the co-author of *Nanovation*, in an interview with Denise Lee Yohn, a brand building expert, [50] *"because of the secrecy surrounding the project, the engineers never really got out with the families on the scooters to find out what they really wanted."* As a result, Tata mistakenly assumed that those people would buy a car that would brand them as poor when in fact, *"many poor people would rather buy a used higher end car than buy a Nano, which would mark them as poor."*[51] Tata also did not appreciate that the purchasing process for buying a car was different to that of buying a scooter. Tata was not close enough to its markets to understand what it would take for markets to switch to the Nano.

Therefore, when innovating within existing trends, putting the customer/market first, would be primordial. An intimate understanding of the job/s that markets would seek to get done, would be important. In the case of habit changing solutions, an understanding of the levers of change/adoption would also be necessary.

What are levers of change/adoption?
Levers of change are the conditions that would need to be met for markets to change their habits. They can be found by identifying the barriers to adoption and by understanding the new jobs that markets would be seeking to get done by changing their habits. For instance, the levers of change for the Nano would have included the following:

1) Brand the Nano as a higher status vehicle over the scooter. For Indians, owning a car is a status symbol – so the Nano should have satisfied that job to be done.
2) Facilitate the buying process. As a matter of fact, some Indians were intimidated to go into a car dealership. Therefore, Tata should have simplified the buying process.

If Tata had been closer to its markets, the Nano could perhaps have been developed to really be the car of the people.

B. Within growing and changing trends:
Identify the forces that will shape or change your market.
Spotting new trends can however pose a different challenge. To start with, you would need to monitor changes at the macro level.

For example:
1) How would changes in the economy impact markets?
2) What new technologies are being commercialised?
3) How would changes in the political arena impact markets?
4) What new laws would impact markets?
5) How would changes in the environment affect markets?
6) How would changes in the demography affect markets?
7) How would changes at the global level affect markets?

For instance, Jeff Bezos spotted that the internet was growing at an exponential rate and that it had started impacting the way that books were purchased. So, he was determined to do business on the internet and he launched Amazon.com.

For *changing trends*, you would need to monitor changes in market habits. For example, are markets becoming more health conscious? Do markets prefer greater convenience? etc. For instance, W.K Kellogg noticed that markets were shifting to a healthier lifestyle when the latter switched from fat laden breakfasts to lighter grain ones.

Today, the use of analytics can help spot growing and changing trends in markets. Analytics offer a snapshot of what's happening in markets. However, analytics cannot explain what new jobs would need to get done due to the advent of growing or changing trends. For instance, data about the increasing number of selfies could not show that markets needed to perform the new job of taking selfies at a distance. It is only by observing markets and by understanding their needs, that selfie stick manufacturers could realise that a selfie stick would be useful to markets.

Analytics cannot also explain why markets would adopt new trends or why they would change their habits. Therefore, the qualitative aspect of research would be needed to shed light on the why's of market behaviour.

Next, it would be important to understand how those growing or changing trends would impact markets, i.e what new jobs would need to get done or what existing jobs would be done differently. For instance, as mentioned earlier, Jeff Bezos successfully identified that the internet had started impacting the way that books were purchased. Consequently, he capitalised on the new trend that was starting to change the way that an existing job was being done and he launched Amazon.

Incidentally, Barnes and Noble could not see the potential of the internet. As a matter of fact, when Amazon started, Barnes and Noble was opening more outlets in shopping malls, and by the time that Amazon had taken on the book industry, it was far too late for the incumbent to catch up. Barnes and Noble never thought of the internet as a medium for selling books. They never analysed how the internet was going to impact markets. Rather, they thought that the internet would be a marketing tool at best.[52]

Therefore, a close monitoring of growing and changing trends would be important, as well as a close observation of markets, in order to understand how those trends would affect existing jobs to be done or would create new jobs to be done.

A question that is often asked is: *Do markets change their habits because of the availability of external solutions or does the change occur endogenously?*

As a matter of fact, it could be both. For instance, health concerns could have caused markets to reduce their consumption of fat laden breakfasts, irrespective of whether there were healthier options available. Equally, the first cereal maker could have introduced the healthier breakfast option and educated markets about the value of adopting a healthier lifestyle, thereby causing a change in market habits towards a healthier lifestyle.

Therefore, it would be important to understand how the markets' needs and tastes would evolve/change, both from within and from their use of external solutions.

C. Ideas that create new trends:
Create new habits in your markets.
Now, take the case of Starbucks. The idea for an espresso bar originated from Howard Schultz's experience in Milan. The idea was highly subjective and it was based on Schultz's assumptions about a

job that the US market might have wanted to get done. In the same line, as will be shown later, Michal Bohanes' idea for Dinnr had created a new job that markets might have wanted to get done, i.e the introduction of variety in everyday cooking. Again, the idea was highly subjective and it was based on Michal Bohanes' own frustrations about his cooking options. Therefore, when looking for new jobs that markets, both general and specific, may want to get done, it would be important that you leverage the experience, knowledge and imagination of as many people as possible. Outside-in and bottom-up approaches would be necessary.

In sum, for ideas that are generated *within existing trends*, an understanding of the job to be done of markets would be of paramount importance. Markets should thus be the foci of observation. For ideas *within growing and changing trends*, while closeness to the market/s would be important, market intelligence about the growth or change in trends would also be useful. Last, for ideas that *create new trends*, being connected to as many 'brains' as possible would be necessary.

It would be important to correctly frame the market impact of an idea because different ideas would carry different layers of uncertainties and rates of adoption and would subsequently need different development, go-to-market and scaling strategies. Beforehand, let's understand in more depth how the value proposition of your idea would impact markets.

EVALUATE THE MARKET IMPACT

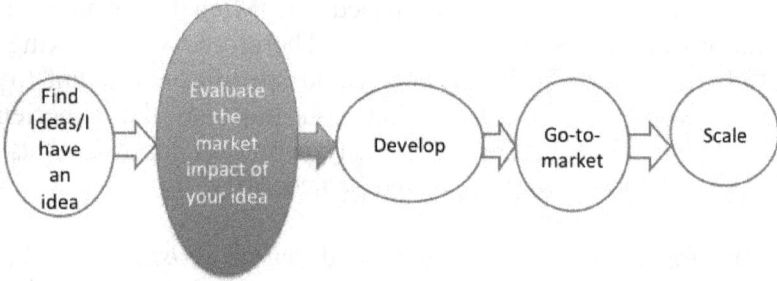

Find Ideas/I have an idea → Evaluate the market impact of your idea → Develop → Go-to-market → Scale

2. Evaluate the market impact of your idea

<u>Key Points</u>:
Identify whether there is:
1) An existing need,
2) A growing need or
3) Whether you are creating a new need for your idea.

The market impact of an idea is usually overlooked by entrepreneurs and innovators. Yet, as will be shown in the following chapters, an understanding of the market impact of an idea would be crucial to the development, commercialisation and scaling of the latter.

For instance, Dinnr assumed that urban professionals were regularly trying to introduce variety in their cooking and were cooking from recipes in order to achieve that purpose. So, its aim was to eliminate the hurdles of cooking from recipes by providing the recipes, the step-by-step instructions and the ingredients.[1]

The question is: *Were markets regularly trying to introduce variety in their cooking?*

Similarly, the Flowtab founders thought that they were solving the pain points experienced by markets when it comes to ordering and paying for drinks in bars.[2] Yet, were they right to operate from such assumptions?

The first step to consider when you have an idea would be to ask the following question:

How does the value proposition of your idea impact markets?

1) Does your idea improve on an existing job to be done? If so, is it solving a pain point or is the improvement based on your subjective perception?

Consider the idea for Danone for instance. In 1919, Isaac Carasso introduced yoghurt in Spain to treat the large number of local children suffering from intestinal disorders.[3] By simply observing and understanding the needs of markets, Carasso came up with a solution and he founded Danone. Likewise, in 1923, Merritt J Osborne developed a new product called Absorbit that cleaned carpets on the spot and eliminated the need for hotels to shut down to clean up. By observing how hotels were cleaned, Merritt Osborne developed a solution that improved on the existing job to be done of cleaning hotels and he founded Ecolab.[4]

Therefore, by studying markets, you would be able to assess whether your idea is addressing an existing job to be done or not. For instance, by observing or interviewing markets, Dinnr could have found out whether markets were trying to introduce variety in their cooking by using recipes.

Usually, the existence of existing solutions would be a first sign that your idea is catering to existing jobs that need to be done. Your challenge would be to determine whether and how your solution would improve on the existing jobs to be done. Thus, by understanding why markets would hire existing solutions and by examining whether they would experience any pain points with respect to existing solutions, you could evaluate whether your idea would have market potential or not. For instance, Flowtab could have found out whether the process of queuing for drinks was a pain point for markets. Through market study, innovators could also get a vague idea of whether the pain points would be big enough that markets would be ready to pay to eliminate them. However, the real test would be to see whether markets would actually pay for the solution. This will be discussed in the next chapter.

Sometimes however, markets may be quite satisfied with an optimum solution and although there would be scope for improvement to existing solutions, markets might not value the improvement that is being offered to the extent that they would pay for it. For instance, as mentioned before, Flowtab improved on the drinks ordering and payment processes in bars. Yet, as it turned out, bar customers did not value the improvement to the existing jobs to be done to the extent of paying for it. The need for an improvement to the existing jobs to be done of ordering and paying for drinks was based on the perception of the Flowtab founders and it was not based on real market insights. Also, Flowtab changed the habits of markets and the founders never investigated what it would take for markets to change their habits. As a result, the idea could not scale.

Therefore, it would be important to determine whether the value proposition associated with the improvement to an existing job to be done, would be based on the pain points or inadequacies actually experienced by markets or on the inadequacies perceived by you.

2) Does your idea improve on an existing job to be done but changes the habits of markets?

An equally important point to look out for would relate to solutions that change the way that an existing job is being done. If by observing or studying markets, you realise that your idea is addressing an existing job to be done, you should find out whether your solution changes the habits of markets. For instance, LinkedIn changed the way that professionals networked. Likewise, in 1997, Netflix considered how the existing trend in the use of the internet could improve on the way that movies were rented. In so doing, it changed the habits of markets. Intuitive Surgical's Da Vinci system for minimally invasive surgery is yet another example of an innovation that improved on the existing job of doing surgery but that changed the habits of markets/ surgeons. Indeed, with the Da Vinci, *"small incisions are used to insert miniaturised wristed instruments and a high definition 3D camera,"*[5] thereby allowing surgeons to perform surgery from a console. Ideas that change market habits would be expected to have a slower take off. The implication of their market impact will be explained in the following chapters.

3) Next, does your idea capitalise on new jobs to be done caused by growing and changing trends or does it capitalise on growing and changing trends that are changing the way that an existing job is done?

For instance, in 2014, many companies capitalised on the changing trend to selfies to launch selfie sticks. The selfie stick was originally invented by Wayne Fromm in 2002, while he was holidaying with his daughter in Florence. For more than a decade, he tried to sell his stick, the Quickpod.[6] However, he could barely trigger interest in his idea. At the time, markets were not trying to take pictures of themselves and Fromm's stick aspired to change the way that an existing job was being done, but it was unsuccessful. However, the changing trend to selfies in the past two years created a need for the selfie stick. Taking selfies at a distance was a new job that markets needed to get done. As a result, the popularity of the selfie stick has grown.

In a similar vein, Stericycle was formed in 1989 to capitalise on the requirements spawned by the Medical Waste Tracking Act that was passed in the USA in 1988.[7] The act changed the way that an existing job was being done - i.e the disposal of medical waste. Indeed, as a consequence of that law, hospitals were required to dispose of medical waste in a way that would render the latter non-infectious prior to disposal. Stericycle provided a cost effective way of managing hospital medical waste and it addressed an existing job that needed to be done in new ways.

So, how would you identify whether your idea is capitalising on a new job to be done or on an existing job that is being done in new ways due to a growing or changing trend?

Usually, a new job to be done or a change in market habit would be spotted through market observation. For example, by observing markets, selfie stick manufacturers could see that taking selfies at a distance was a new job that markets needed to get done.

A close monitoring of changes at the macro level would also be important. For example, an awareness of the new legislation pertaining to the disposal of medical waste, led to the creation of Stericyle. Market intelligence about the trends would also be useful in understanding the rate at which the trends are growing or changing respectively.

4) Last, does your idea create a new job that markets may want to get done?

Jobs that markets may want to get done are those that markets are not actively trying to satisfy. For example, enjoying the romance of espresso in a neighbourhood place was not a job that markets were seeking to get done. It was a job that they might have wanted to get done. Starbucks created a new job that markets might have wanted to get done and it had fifty percent chance of being adopted. Likewise, having breakfast was not a job that breakfast skippers were trying to get done. It was a job that they might or might not have wanted to get done. Yet, the idea took off and today, Mondelez international has created a new trend in breakfast biscuits. The success of both companies rested on the willingness of markets to adopt the new jobs to be done.

Thus, if you have an idea and are not sure whether it is creating a new job that markets may want to get done, market study would help you clarify that aspect. For instance, if you had been in Howard Schultz's shoes at the time that he had the idea for a coffee bar, by studying markets, you could have found out whether they were seeking to enjoy the romance of espresso in a safe neighbourhood place. If they had been, then Howard Schultz's idea would have been addressing an existing job to be done. If not, the idea would have been creating a job that markets might have wanted to get done.

A classification of the ideas of the Forbes 2014[8] one hundred most innovative companies in the world showed that ideas fell into each one of the categories mentioned. The rationale for understanding how ideas would impact markets would lie in the fact that they would need different development, go-to-market and scaling strategies.

The next chapter will show how different ideas would need different development strategies.

DEVELOP

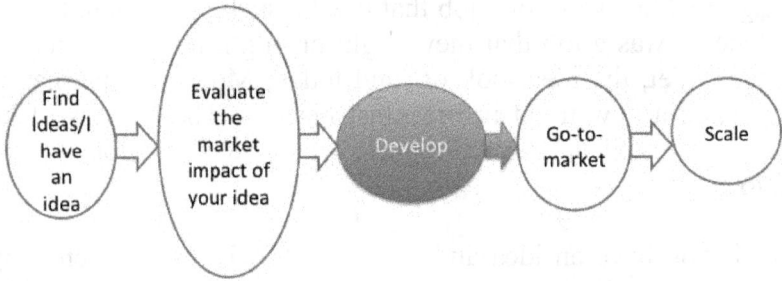

3. Develop your idea

Key Points:
1) Map out the layers of uncertainties.
2) Eliminate those uncertainties.

A start-up's journey would usually provide a good insight into the process of bringing new ideas to market. The main tension that innovators and entrepreneurs would usually face is the following:

How does one bring new ideas to market, under conditions of uncertainty?

For instance, Dinnr was created based on the belief that young urban professionals (young couples and young families) were seeking to introduce variety in their cooking and were regularly cooking from recipes in order to achieve that aim. However, after fifteen months, the company closed down because it did not have enough traction.

Likewise, the Flowtab founders thought that queuing in bars and ordering drinks were pain points that were big enough that markets would pay to eliminate them. However, after two years, the company had to close down because it had only 12 regular users across 9 bars.

Question is: *Could those entrepreneurs/innovators have done anything differently to overcome their uncertainties?*

It is axiomatic that innovators would face some level of uncertainty when commercialising new ideas. The main uncertainty would pertain to whether markets would adopt the new idea. And anyone who is familiar with Eric Ries' *Lean Start-Up* would know that one way of overcoming that uncertainty would be to develop a minimum viable product (MVP) that would give early feedback on the market's reaction.[1] A minimum viable product is a primitive version of a product or solution, which is designed to give feedback on the market's reaction in the shortest possible amount of time and at the lowest cost. For example, when Groupon first started, their minimum viable product consisted of a WordPress blog, a pizza coupon and handmade PDF's, and every day they would write a new post about the offers and would send the PDF coupons to buyers by email.[2]

Yet, if you study past innovations, you would find that different types of innovations carried other uncertainties as well, that went beyond the market's reactions. As a result, different tools were needed to eliminate those uncertainties. Furthermore, the MVP would eliminate different types of uncertainties for different types of ideas and these will be explored on the following pages.

3.1 Map out the layers of uncertainties

Within Existing Trends

The Google story
To begin with, when Larry Page and Sergei Brin developed their Page Ranking Technology, they wanted to improve on existing search functions.

The layers of uncertainties for the budding company were as follows:

Layers Of Uncertainties For Google's Search Engine

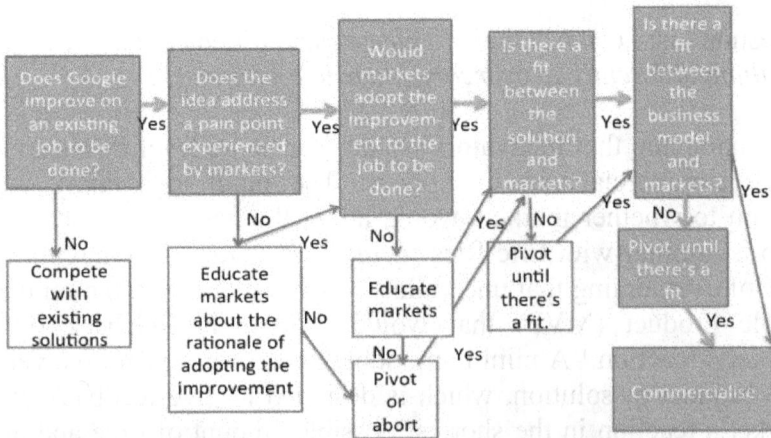

TOOLS TO ELIMINATE THOSE UNCERTAINTIES
Market Study - The Google founders were heavy users of search engines,

so they were intimately familiar with the pain points associated with existing search engines.

MVP - Google's beta test showed that markets were ready to adopt the idea. It also ensured that that there was a fit between the solution and markets. However, the founders should have experimented with different business models much earlier. As a matter of fact, they persisted with only one business model and for a long time, they could not generate cash.

Being heavy users of search engines, the Google founders were aware of the pain points that markets were experiencing with respect to existing search engines. They thus capitalised on an existing job to be done of internet search and came up with a solution that was superior to existing ones.

Then, in order to overcome the uncertainties pertaining to the fit between the solution and markets, Brin and Page beta tested their search engine on the Stanford campus, prior to its launch and its popularity grew among students and professors.[3] As John Hennessy, a top computer scientist who is president of Stanford University,[4] recalled, when Google's search engine was brought to his attention in the mid 1990's, he typed his own name in the search box. *"And the first thing that came up was Stanford University and that didn't happen in other search engines."*[5] Google significantly improved on the job to be done of internet search and the beta test as well as the increased popularity of the technology validated both the market's appreciation of the improvement to the job to be done of internet search and the fit between the search engine and the market. As a matter of fact, within one and a half years, the search engine went from handling 10000 queries a day to 15m in 2000.[6] However, for a long time, the start-up could not find a viable business model. Their initial plan was to license their technology to other companies. But except for Red Hat and Netscape, no other company wanted to license the technology.[7] Here, Google should perhaps have experimented with different business models at the outset.

Next, consider how the Ipod was developed.
As mentioned earlier, the iPod improved on an existing job to be done of listening to music on the go. The iPod was created because Apple thought *"they could bring a better mp3 player to market."*[8]

Thus, in February 2001, the company approached Tony Fadell, an inventor and designer, to discuss the possibility of creating a prototype. Fadell studied markets and spoke with everyone in the handheld industry. He also studied competitors' products.[9] And at the end of his contract, he had three prototypes to show to Steve Jobs. Apple's senior Vice President of product marketing, Phil Schiller, also presented prototypes with the scroll wheel. Schiller thought that the plus and minus buttons of existing mp3 players at the time were "*tedious*" and that the scroll wheel would be a better option for a player with 1000 songs.[10]

If we map out the layers of uncertainties for the iPod, they would be as follows:

Layers Of Uncertainties For Apple's IPod

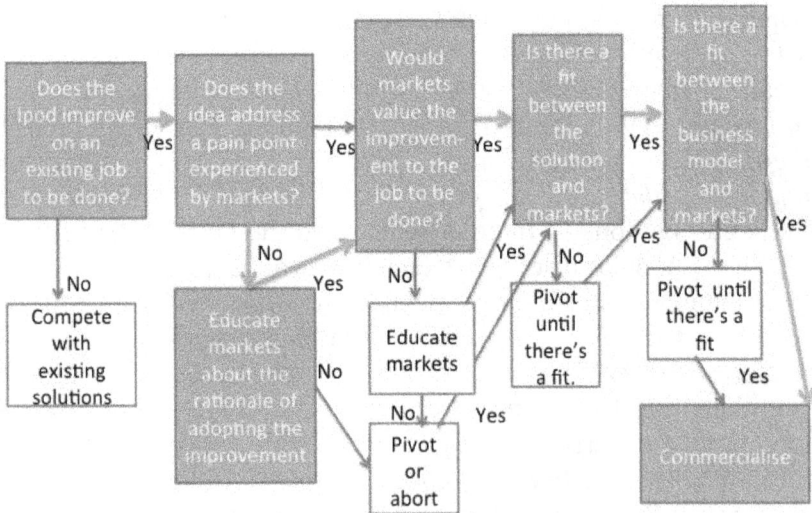

TOOLS TO ELIMINATE THOSE UNCERTAINTIES

Market Study: Apple studied existing mp3 players and they thought that they could come up with a better product that would hold more songs, would be better looking and would be easier to use. However, the improvement to the job to be done of listening to music on the go was more based on Apple's subjective perception rather than derived from market insights. Therefore, Apple had to educate markets about the value of using the iPod.

MVP/ Prototype: Normally, Apple should have used a prototype to test the market's reaction to its product but the prototype was tested by the Apple team only, and it was given the final seal of approval by Steve Jobs. Apple wanted to bring to market a finished product. They thought that they knew what markets would like and in this case, they ended up being right. However, they could have been wrong, as will be shown later by the Flowtab and Segway examples. The MVP would have also shown whether there was a fit between the product and markets and between the business model and markets.

Here it can be noted that although the iPod improved on an existing job to be done of listening to music on the go, the improvement was based on the subjective perception of the Apple team. At its launch, the iPod was met with huge criticism from the press and analysts. But markets ended up appreciating its superior design and performance, and by September 2012, 350 million iPods had been sold.[11]

Apple discovered its market's reactions to the improvement in the job to be done of listening to music on the go, at the iPod's launch. The company also discovered whether there was a fit between the product and markets and between the business model and markets. However, it could have learnt about the market's reactions much earlier using an MVP/prototype. Luckily, markets ended up loving the product. As will be shown later, other inventions such as Flowtab and the Segway were less fortunate.

Now, let's examine the layers of uncertainties for ideas that change the habits of markets within existing trends.

Salesforce.com's Software as a Service changed the habits of markets.
Consider Salesforce.com's online software as a service (SaaS) for instance. Marc Benioff's SaaS idea entailed a change in the way that an existing job was being done, i.e use of CRM software. The layers of uncertainties for the idea were as follows:

Layers Of Uncertainties For Salesforce.Com's SaaS

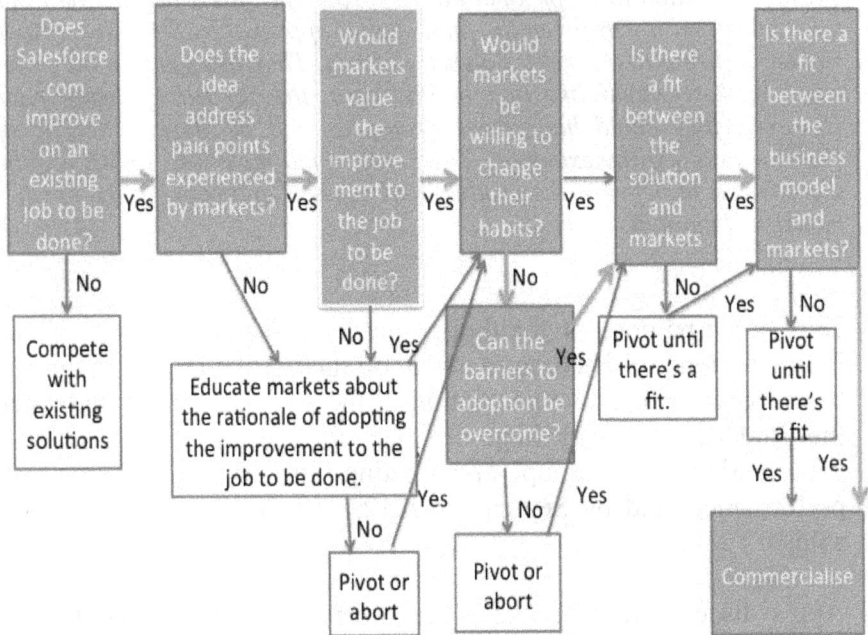

TOOLS TO ELIMINATE THOSE UNCERTAINTIES:

Market Study: Benioff had worked in the software industry for many years and he knew the pain points that markets were experiencing with respect to enterprise software. In addition, he invited his former colleagues at Cisco to share what markets did not like about traditional enterprise software.[12]

MVP/ Prototype: The early prototype helped identify the barriers to adoption namely that no one wanted to be first to take the huge risk of putting their data on Salesforce.com's server. The MVP also ensured that there was a fit between the solution and markets and a fit between the business model and markets.

In order to eliminate the uncertainty pertaining to the fit between the solution and markets, Benioff invited his friends and former colleagues at Cisco to meet at his apartment and offer feedback on the prototype.[13] His friends also *"shared what markets experienced when using traditional enterprise software."*[14] By eliminating the pain points experienced by markets, Benioff thought that the latter would be more receptive to the improvement to the existing job to be done of managing CRM, which he was proposing.

The willingness of markets to change their habits still had to be ascertained. At that stage, it was important to identify the barriers to adoption. One main barrier was the reluctance of markets to put their proprietary data on Salesforce.com's server. No one wanted to be the first to take a giant risk. [15] The company thus targeted *"pioneers who saw an opportunity to participate in something new and exciting."*[16] To gain a foothold in the market and to ensure product-market fit, the company offered the software for free to five pilot customers and they used the insights of the customers to develop the application.[17] It may be worth noting here, that Salesforce.com developed its application closely with markets, identifying the barriers to the market's change in habits and ensuring that the application provided more value to markets than conventional software did.

During its first year in operation in 1999, the company acquired 1500 customers. That figure increased by 2000 the following year and then by 2200 the year after. However from 2003 to 2004, there was a sharp increase of 5200 followed by 6600 the next year and 9300 the year after. Clearly, adoption was slow in the beginning but it eventually gained momentum in the market.[18]

In comparison, consider the Rivet and Sway story.
Rivet and Sway was an online retailer that specialised in prescription eyeglasses for women. It was founded in 2011, and targeted *"time strapped women who could not stand the shopping experience."*[19]

The layers of uncertainties for the company were as follows:

Layers Of Uncertainties For Rivet and Sway

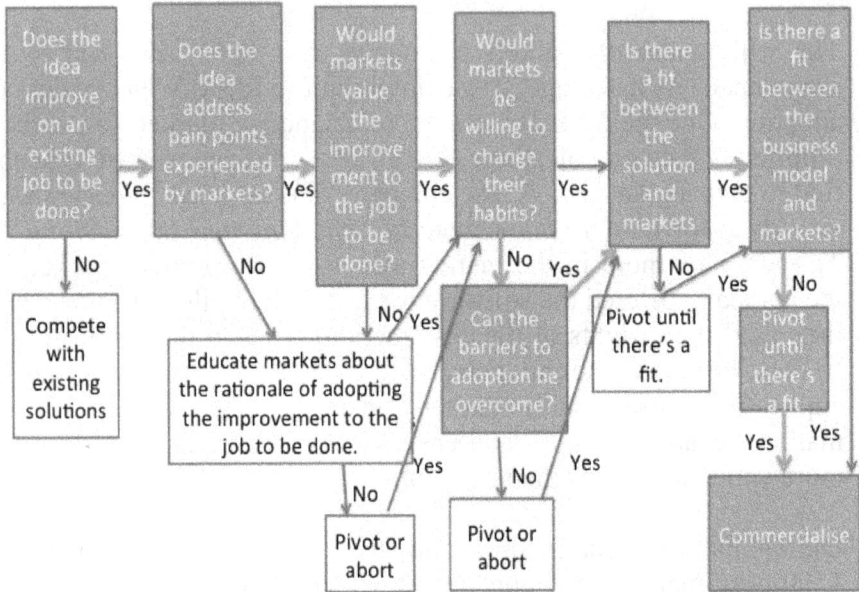

TOOLS TO OVERCOME THE UNCERTAINTIES

Market Research/ Study: John Lusk, one of the co-founders, studied the target market to understand the pain points that women experienced when buying glasses.[20] Some of the pain points that women experienced were that they did not have the time to shop and they could not stand the shopping experience.

MVP: Would have determined whether markets were ready to adopt the service. It would have also helped in identifying the barriers to adoption. Equally, the MVP would have allowed the company to gauge whether there was a fit between the solution and markets and between the business model and markets.

In an interview with Business Insider, one of the co-founders, John Lusk, explained that prior to the launch of the company, they did *"tons of research to determine all the pain points that women experience when trying to buy glasses,"* and they *"structured their offer accordingly."*[21]

However, Sarah Bryar, the CEO who was later appointed in 2013, explained that *"women wanted to try frames on before purchasing and it was an expensive marketing program to ship frames back and forth."*[22] If it had used an MVP, the start-up could have identified the barriers to adoption much earlier. The MVP would have also ensured that there was a fit between the business model and markets. As a result of its high cost of acquiring customers, and because it could not secure additional funding, the company closed down in 2014.[23] Had they eliminated their uncertainties prior to commercialisation, perhaps Rivet and Sway could have pivoted their strategies earlier.

Next, take a look at the Segway story.
The Segway impacted its market in very much the same way that Salesforce.com's SaaS and Rivet and Sway impacted theirs, i.e it addressed an existing job to be done but it changed the habits of markets.

The Segway was designed to revolutionise travel within cities. Its inventor, Dean Kamen, thought that *"the Segway would be to cars what cars were to the horse and buggy."*[24] Yet, the idea did not gain much traction once it was commercialised and part of the reason was that Kamen did not overcome the uncertainties associated with his invention, prior to commercialisation. He took market acceptance for granted based on his own perception of how the market would value the improvement to the job to be done of transport within cities.

Since the Segway also changed the habits of markets, Kamen should have tried to identify the barriers to adoption and he should have co-created with markets to ensure product-market fit. Instead, the Segway was kept under heavy wraps until its commercialisation and when it was unveiled, it did not have the impact that its founder was anticipating. (See chapter 5 for full story)

If we map out the layers of uncertainties for the company, they would be as follows:

Layers Of Uncertainties For The Segway

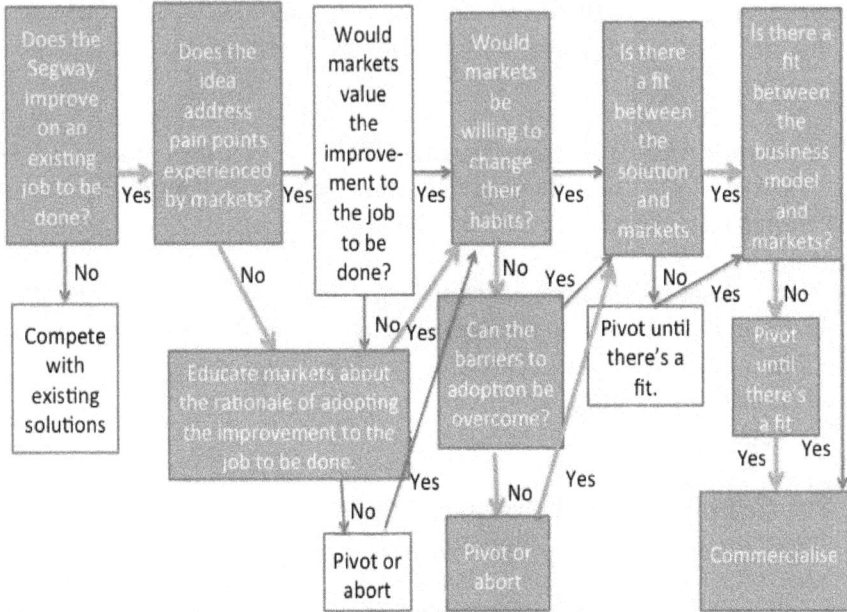

TOOLS TO ELIMINATE THE UNCERTAINTIES

Market research/study: Dean Kamen should have found out whether markets were experiencing any pain points with respect to existing modes of transport. Instead, the Segway was invented based on Dean Kamen's subjective improvement of transport within cities. Therefore, Kamen should have educated markets about the value of riding a Segway.

MVP: An MVP would have helped determine whether markets were ready to adopt the idea. It would have also identified the barriers to adoption and would have ensured that there was a fit between the product and markets and between the business model and markets.

Similarly, the Nano was developed in complete isolation from its markets. And although it had lots of pre-orders, its success did not last.

Layers Of Uncertainties For The Nano

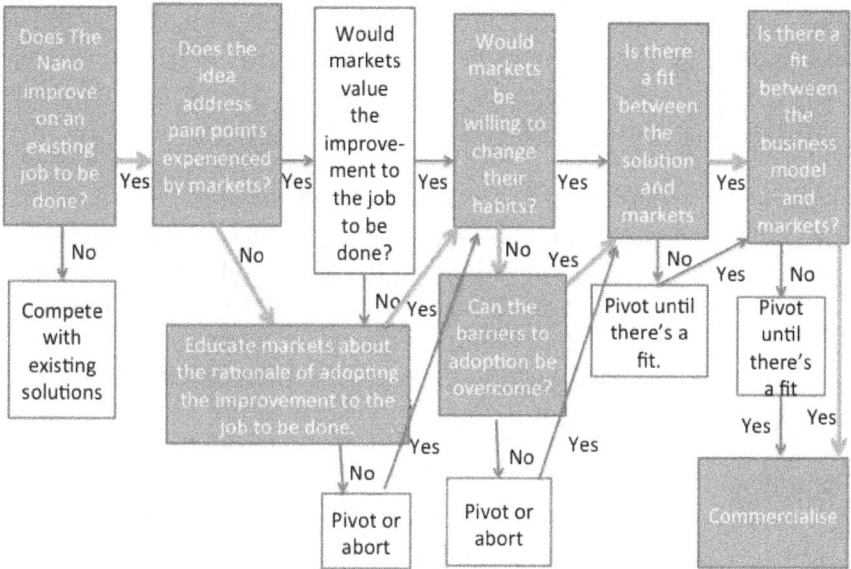

TOOLS TO ELIMINATE THE UNCERTAINTIES

Market Research/Study: Would have allowed Tata to understand whether they were addressing the pain points of markets.

MVP: An MVP would have shown whether the pain points were big enough that markets would have adopted the idea. It would have also allowed Tata to identify the barriers to adoption and it would have ensured that there was a fit between the Nano and markets and between the business model and markets.

Here, it may be worth noting that both the Segway and the Nano improved on existing jobs to be done of markets but the improvements were more based on the subjective perception of the innovators than derived from market insights. Indeed, Tata never tried to gauge whether markets wanted to eliminate the pain points associated with scooter travel. Likewise, Kamen never tried to find out whether markets wanted to eliminate the pain points associated with transport within cities. Also, neither Kamen nor Tata tried to identify the barriers to adoption. They went straight to the commercialisation stage.

When innovating within existing trends, eliminating pain points that markets would experience with respect to existing solutions could increase the chances that markets would value the improvement to their existing job to be done. Therefore, studying markets and understanding the problems that they would experience when trying to perform a job, could eliminate to some extent the uncertainty associated with market adoption.

However, as mentioned in the previous chapter, the more subjective the improvement to an existing job to be done is, i.e the more it is based on your perception of how an existing job to be done could be improved as opposed to being derived from market insights, the higher would the uncertainty relating to market adoption be. Therefore, you would need to promote the value associated with the improvement to the job to be done. Also, if the ideas change the habits of markets, you would need to identify the barriers to adoption.

Now, consider the uncertainties that ideas within growing and changing trends would carry.

Within growing and changing trends

How Salesforce.com developed Platform as A Service (PaaS).
Salesforce.com capitalised on the new job to be done spawned by the changing trend to Software as a Service (SaaS), to launch Platform as a Service (PaaS). With the changing trend to software as an online service, markets needed a platform that would allow them to both create and host their own software online. As Benioff recounts, *"customers were clamouring for more applications and we didn't have the resources to build everything ourselves."*[25] The growth in SaaS had created a new job that needed to be done, i.e an online structure to host different enterprise applications. As a result, Salesforce.com launched Platform as a Service (PaaS).

The advantage for Salesforce.com was that it knew who its users would be and could thus provide more targeted solutions and marketing that in turn could help drive adoption. As a matter of fact, PaaS was successfully embraced by Salesforce.com's *"customers and partners."*[26] During its first year in existence, Force.com (the online platform) hosted 85000 new applications. The year after, in 2009, the number increased to 110000 and in 2010, they had 185000 new applications showing rapid adoption.[27] Here, adoption of PaaS was dependent on the growth in SaaS. The company knew that they had a critical mass of users who were using SaaS and so they could safely launch PaaS.

Layers Of Uncertainties For Salesforce.com PaaS

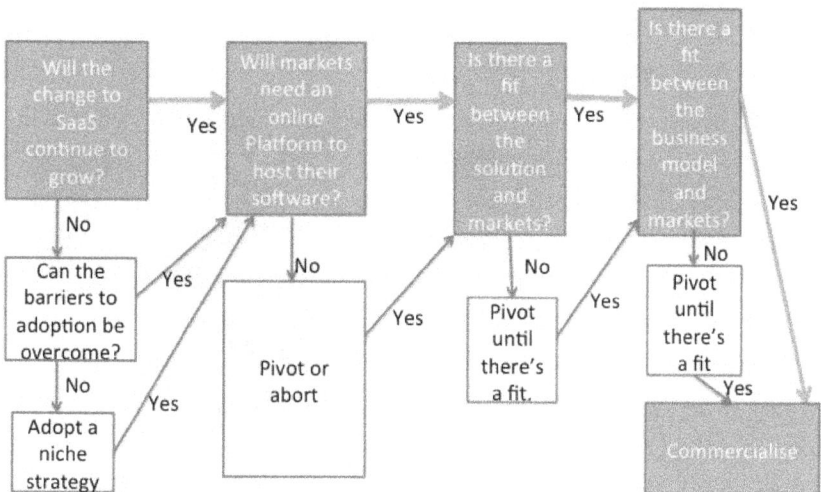

TOOLS TO ELIMINATE THE UNCERTAINTIES

Market data: Benioff knew that SaaS had a critical mass of users who were ready to use PaaS.

Market observation: Closeness to markets allowed Salesforce.com to notice that markets were asking for more applications and that an online platform was needed to host those applications.

Prototype/ MVP: Allowed the company to understand whether there was a fit between the solution and markets and between the business model and markets.

Similarly, Netscape capitalised on a new job to be done that resulted from the growing use of the internet. The World Wide Web had created the need for an internet browser and Netscape provided the first user-friendly browser. The success of Netscape was directly proportional to the growth in the use of the internet. Unsurprisingly, within the first two weeks of the Netscape 1.0 release, the company sold $ 365000's worth of product.[28] In the second quarter, sales reached nearly $ 12 million [29] and by mid 1996, the company had realised a profit of $4.7 million.[30] Were it not for competition from Microsoft, Netscape would have expanded its hegemony as the internet became more ubiquitous.

Layers Of Uncertainties For Netscape

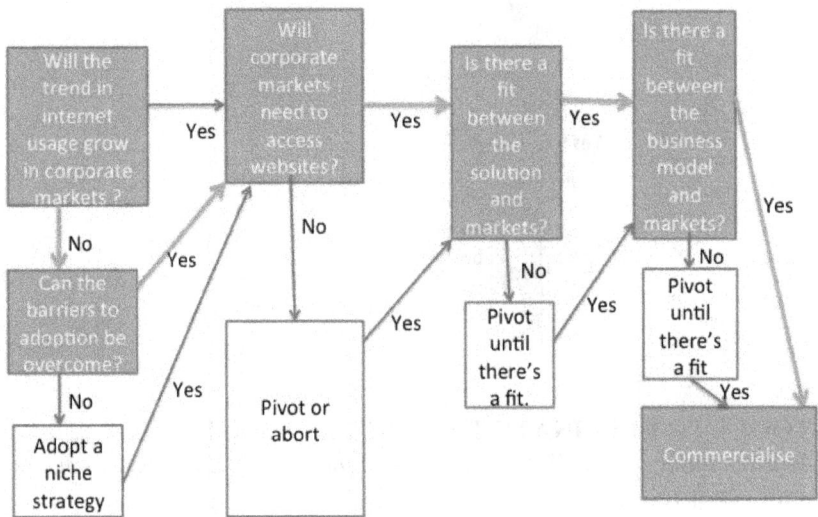

TOOLS TO ELIMINATE UNCERTAINTIES
Market intelligence: Netscape did not have data about the growth in internet usage. However, with the creation of the Mosaic browser, it "became clear at the Wizards Workshop that the entire landscape of the World Wide Web, would shift.[31]

Market study: Market study allowed the company to understand that corporate markets would embrace the internet only if they had a clear idea of how to sell online.[32]

MVP: When a beta version of Mosaic was loaded on one of NCSA's public servers, within 10 minutes, someone downloaded it. Within thirty minutes, one hundred people had it and "in less than an hour they were getting feedback via Email from excited users around the world.[33]

Now, let's examine the layers of uncertainties for ideas that change the way that existing jobs are done within growing and changing trends.

How Amazon developed its online retail website.
Take a look at Amazon.com for instance. Jeff Bezos spotted a growing trend in the use of the internet and he noticed that the internet was starting to change the way that books were bought. Internet technology was new at the time and people had just started buying books online. Already cognizant of the facts that internet usage was growing at the rate of 2300% per year and that books were the most sold items on the internet, Bezos decided to launch an online bookstore.[34] However, the level of uncertainty facing the company was quite high.

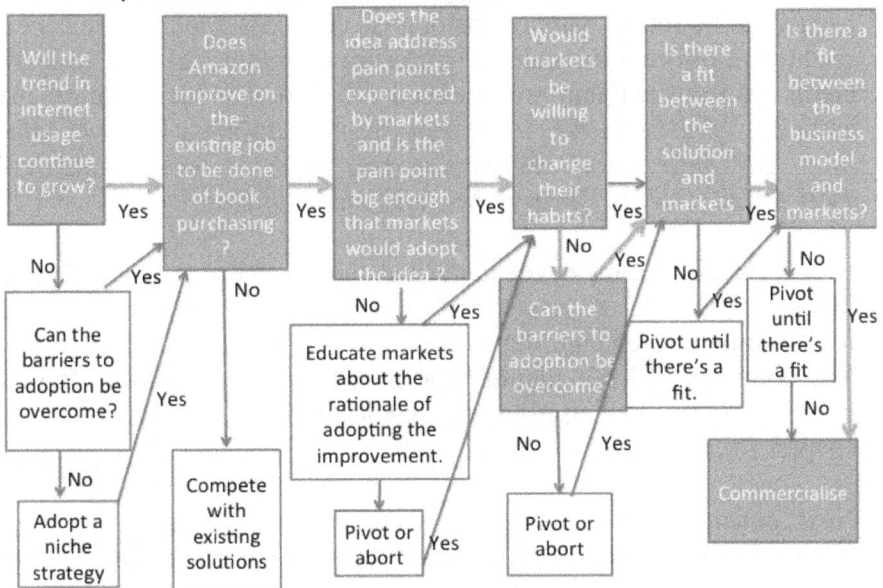

Layers of Uncertainties For Amazon's Online Retail Website

TOOLS TO ELIMINATE THE UNCERTAINTIES:

Market intelligence: Indicated the rate at which the internet was growing. It also showed that books were starting to be sold online.

Market observation: Showed that there were already two players on the market namely Clbooks.com and Books.com and that markets had already started changing their book purchasing habits.

MVP: Identified the barriers to adoption. It also ensured that there was a fit between the solution and markets and between the business model and markets.

To start with, it wasn't clear whether book buyers would continue adopting the internet and if so, whether they would change their book purchasing habits. In that respect, Amazon relied on market intelligence to gauge the rate at which internet usage was growing.

Also, by observing markets, Jeff Bezos could find that there were already two online booksellers on the market and that markets had already started changing their book purchasing habits.

Then, Amazon's beta test prior to its launch helped identify the barriers to adoption namely customers' concerns about storing their credit card information online.[35] Amazon thus came up with a secure credit card system that was dubbed CC Motel.[36] Incidentally, the company *"finished 1996, its first full year in business with net sales of $ 15.7 million- an attention getting 3000 per cent jump over 1995's $ 511000."*[37] Clearly, the trend had caught on.

In contrast, Boo.com never identified the growth rate in the use of the internet in the UK. Also, they did not consider what it would take for customers to change their habits to shopping for fashion online. The company did not identify the barriers to adoption and it was more focused on scaling. As a result, it did not survive.[38] (See chapter 5 for full story)

Next, consider how Kellogg's cereal came into being.
Kellogg's cereal was developed when W.K Kellogg noticed that markets were shifting to a healthier lifestyle and were changing their breakfast habits from *"fat laden ones to lighter grain ones."*[39] Kellogg also discovered that a much better cereal could be produced

when only the *"sweetheart of the corn or corn grit"* was used.[40] As a result, the company became a leader in the breakfast cereal market.

If we map out the layers of uncertainties for the cereal, they would be as follows:

Layers of Uncertainties For Kellogg's Cereal

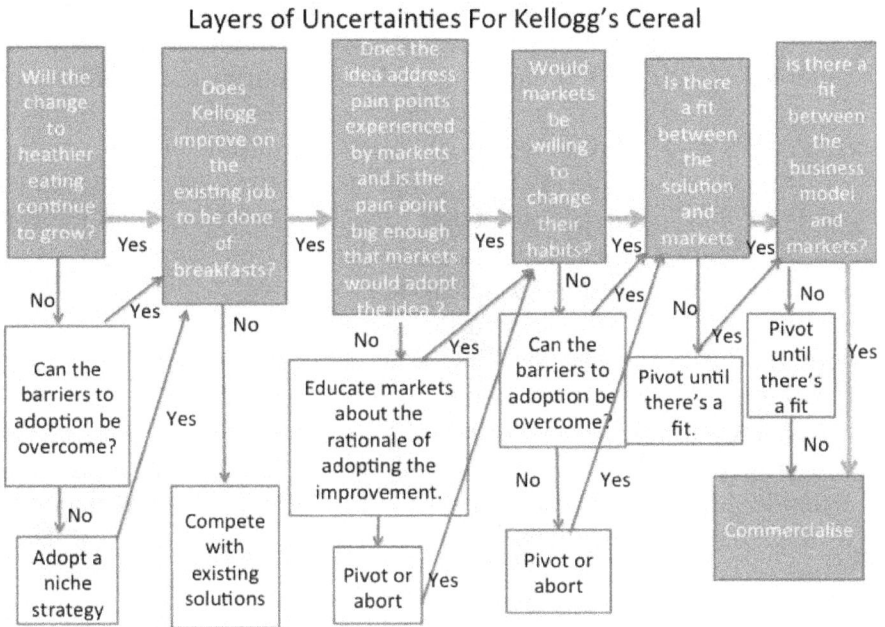

TOOLS TO ELIMINATE THE UNCERTAINTIES:
Market intelligence: Would have allowed Kellogg to gauge whether the shift to a healthier lifestyle would continue to grow.

Market observation: W.K Kellogg actually noticed that markets were shifting their habits from fat laden breakfasts to lighter grain ones. There were already few players in the breakfast cereal market in Michigan and a study of competitors' products allowed Kellogg to come up with a better product.

MVP/Prototype: Would have allowed Kellogg to discover further barriers to adoption. It would have also ensured that there was a fit between the product and markets and between the business model and markets.

Next, for ideas that create new trends, the layers of uncertainties would be different as well.

Create new trends

How Howard Schultz tested the Starbucks idea.

Take the case of Starbucks for instance. Unlike the other innovators, Howard Schultz innovated from a different angle. He wanted to import the espresso bar concept from Italy to the United States. Thus, he imagined a job that the US market might have wanted to get done, i.e enjoy the romance of coffee in a coffee bar. Problem for Schultz, however, was that the idea itself carried a high level of uncertainty as he had no means of knowing from the outset, whether the American people would adopt the new job to be done. Furthermore, Schultz's market was undefined and he couldn't gauge potential market reaction. Therefore, his only option was to test the idea/ new job to be done as cheaply as possible. After a successful test marketing, Schultz opened Il Giornale (which was later merged with Starbucks).[41] On the first day in 1986, it had nearly 300 customers.[42] Within 6 months they were serving more than 1000 customers a day.[43] Starbucks created a new trend in the lives of the American people and people adopted the new job to be done. Rate of idea adoption was proportional to the rate at which the market was willing /persuaded to adopt the new trend.

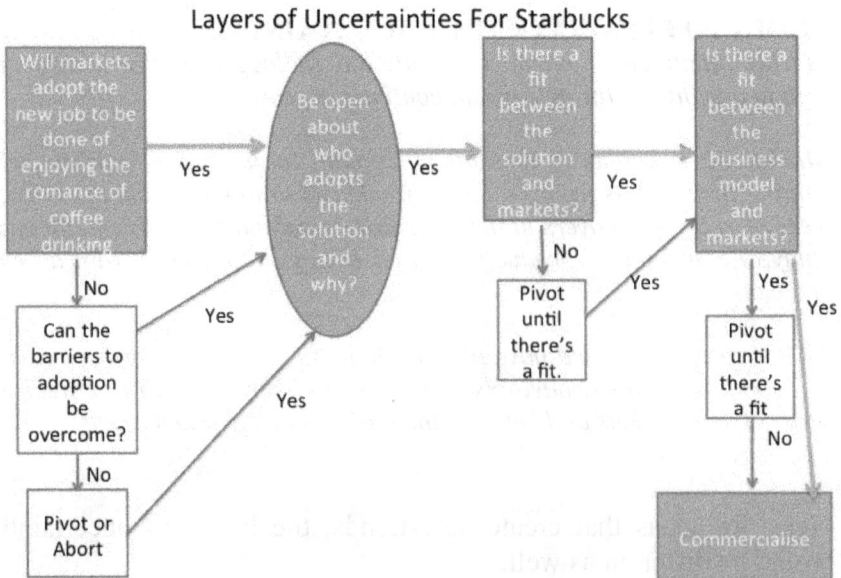

Layers of Uncertainties For Starbucks

TOOL TO ELIMINATE THE UNCERTAINTIES
MVP: Identified whether markets would adopt the new job to be done. It also allowed the company to understand its growing market and to tailor the solution to what markets needed and to achieve a fit with markets both in terms of solution and business model.

Not unlike Starbucks, Mondelez International imagined a job that people who usually skip breakfast, might have wanted to get done, namely that of eating breakfast. Here, the uncertainties pertained to whether the 'breakfast skippers' would actually warm up to the 'job' of eating breakfast and would 'hire' biscuits as the solution. As opposed to Starbucks however, Mondelez International knew who its potential market was. As such, the company could try to understand its market before launching its product. It could also provide more targeted advertising to help speed up adoption. In the UK for instance, at Belvita's launch, the TV ad for Belvita biscuits featured a busy radio presenter eating Belvita in the morning and lasting until lunch. According to *Ingredients Network.com Insights*, the market penetration of breakfast biscuits grew from 6% to 11% in 2011 and rose to 17% in 2012.[44].

Layers of Uncertainties For Belvita Biscuits

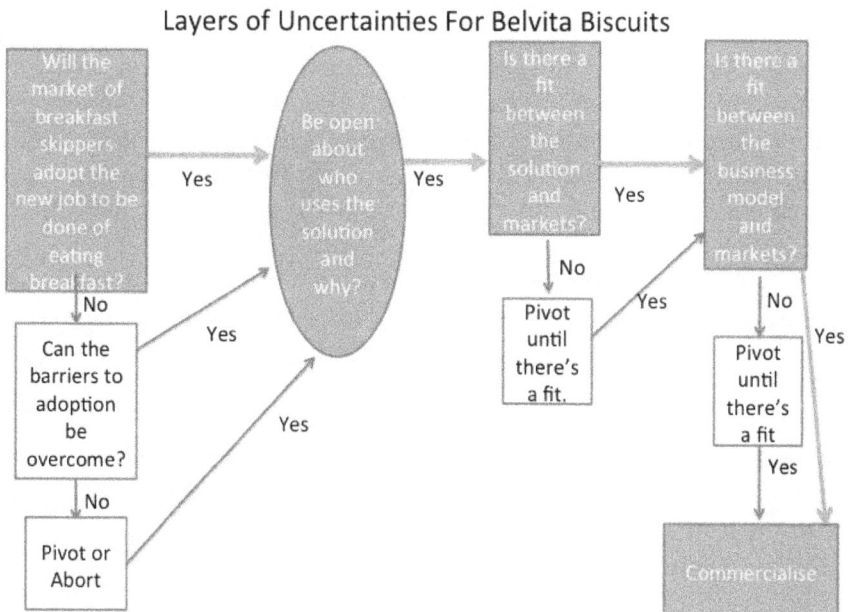

When creating new trends, the first uncertainty that you would face would pertain to whether markets would adopt the new job to be done.

In the case of Starbucks, the question was: *Would markets be happy to enjoy the "romance" of drinking espresso in a social setting?*

In the case of Belvita biscuits, the question was: *Would breakfast skippers be happy to eat breakfast?*

At that stage, you must look at who interacts with your solution and why. Often, an idea that creates a job that markets may want to get done could end up fulfilling other needs. Taking the case of Starbucks, although initially, the company wanted markets to adopt the new job of enjoying the romance of espresso, Starbucks ended up fulfilling other jobs to be done as well. For instance, entrepreneurs go there to work sometimes. Some people use it as an informal place to conduct meetings. Other people go there to read and write. The jobs to be done that Starbucks fulfils today are more varied than the job that Howard Schultz initially set out to create. Likewise, markets buy Belvita biscuits for perhaps various reasons. For instance, it could be a good pre-gym snack or a snack for afternoon tea.

The second source of uncertainty would pertain to the fit between the solution and budding markets, i.e, do markets like what you are offering? For instance, markets could have been happy adopting the job of enjoying the romance of espresso, but what if they thought that the coffee tasted too bitter? Similarly, breakfast skippers might have been happy having breakfast but was breakfast biscuit a good solution?

The third source of uncertainty would relate to the viability of the business model. How can the innovator extract value from the idea? Would markets pay for the solution? If so, how much?

It can thus be seen that different types of ideas would have different sources of uncertainties. Different tools have also been used to eliminate the different types of uncertainties. Those tools will be further examined on the following pages.

3.2 Tools to eliminate uncertainties

A. The Minimum Viable Product (MVP)

The concept of the Minimum Viable Product (MVP) was popularised by Eric Ries in the *Lean Start-Up*. The MVP is a primitive version of a product/service that is designed to give early feedback on the markets' reactions at the lowest cost and in the shortest amount of time possible. Usually innovators and entrepreneurs would spend a huge amount of time and resources perfecting a solution, only to find out about real market reactions when the solution is actually commercialised. E.g. The Segway, the Nano and Flowtab to name just a few. Therefore, an MVP can shorten that process, allowing innovators to effectively learn from actual market reactions and change their solution or their strategies where needed. However, the MVP would eliminate only certain types of uncertainties and it would have different uses based on how an idea would impact markets.

Within existing trends

For instance, if as Google's search engine, your idea improves on an existing job to be done and if it addresses pain points experienced by markets, the MVP would show whether the pain points experienced by markets would be big enough that markets would actually adopt the idea or would pay for it. The MVP would also ensure that there is a fit between your solution and what markets are looking for. Equally, it will ensure that there is a fit between the business model and markets.

Next, if as Salesforce.com's SaaS, your solution changes the habits of markets, the MVP would also allow you to identify the barriers to adoption early in the process.

Take the case of Amazon's Echo for instance. Echo improves on the job that markets seek to get done by asking for assistance from intelligent personal assistants and knowledge navigators such as Siri and Cortana.[45]

Amazon launched a beta version of Echo and reviews seemed to suggest that Echo did not do much more than other virtual assistants except perhaps for the fact that it comes in the form of a cylindrical device that operates wirelessly at home. Thus, it can be placed anywhere in a room and anyone can ask it/her (Alexa) for a question or a task.[46] Since the improvement to the job to be done of digital personal assistance was more based on Amazon's subjective perception than derived from market insights, Amazon educated the market about the value of having a live-in wireless digital assistant. As a matter of fact, in Echo's ad, the product is positioned as an assistant to the family as a whole.[47]

Echo also changes the habits of markets and with a beta version of the digital assistant, Amazon could spot privacy concerns of markets. At Echo's launch, the company made clear that the device could only be activated with the wake word "Alexa" and that the microphone on the device could be physically switched off as well.[48]

If we map out the the layers of uncertainties for Echo, they would be as follows:

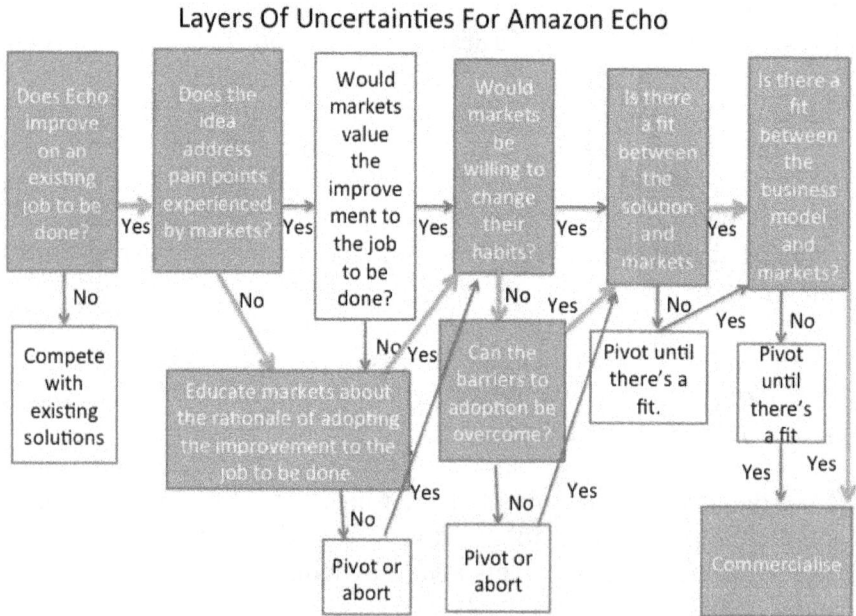

Layers Of Uncertainties For Amazon Echo

- Echo did not address the pain points experienced by markets, therefore, Amazon had to educate markets about the value of having a live-in digital assistant.

Then the **MVP/beta version** identified:
- Whether markets were willing to change their habits.
- Whether the barriers to adoption could be overcome.
- Whether there was a fit between the solution and markets.
- Whether there was a fit between the business model and markets.

Within growing and changing trends
Now, within growing and changing trends, there are certain uncertainties that cannot be eliminated with an MVP. For instance, when Amazon's online retail website was first created, it capitalised on a growing trend in the use of the internet. As shown earlier, one of its uncertainties pertained to whether usage of the internet would grow. Therefore, the company had to rely on market intelligence to eliminate those uncertainties. In contrast, Boo.com, the online fashion retail company, did not realise that the internet penetration in the UK was only 20%.[49] Had they used market intelligence, they would probably have operated more cautiously.

An MVP however ensured that there was a fit between the solution and markets and between the business model and markets. For instance, during the late spring of 1995, Amazon asked several hundred friends to *"put the system through its paces by browsing for books and making pretend purchases"* and by the time that they launched, they *"knew that they had already ironed out ninety eight percent of the glitches."*[50]

For *growing and changing trends* that *change the way that existing jobs are done,* an MVP would also identify the barriers to adoption. Thus, when Amazon first beta tested its online retail website, it found out that markets were fearful of storing their credit card details online. As a result, the company came up with a secure payment system that ensured that people would adopt the new service.[51]

Therefore, when innovating within growing and changing trends, access to market intelligence would be important as well as feedback from an MVP.

Creating new trends
Next, when creating *new jobs that markets may want to get done*, the MVP would serve different purposes.

First, it will indicate whether markets would be happy to adopt the new job to be done. Then, it will give an early indication of who interacts with the solution and why. Indeed, as mentioned earlier, often, an idea that creates a job that markets may want to get done, could end up fulfilling different needs. For example, markets do not go to Starbucks to enjoy the romance of drinking espresso only. Starbucks fulfils several other jobs to be done. For example, entrepreneurs and students often go there to work and study respectively. Some people go there to read. Others go there to have coffee with friends. So, the original concept ended up fulfilling different needs. Therefore, for trend creating ideas, an MVP can help innovators better understand the markets that their solutions would create.

In light of the above examples, it can be seen that an MVP would have different uses for different types of ideas. Therefore, it would be important to first understand the market impact of your idea and to then understand what you should look for from the MVP.

The second tool that innovators would usually use to eliminate uncertainties is market research. However it would be worth understanding the role of market research in the innovation process.

B. Market Research/Study

Within existing trends
Within existing trends, market research would help understand the jobs that markets would seek to get done. Studying markets would also reveal how existing solutions would fall short of existing jobs to be done.

For instance, recently on the Apprentice show in the UK, one of the contestants, Bianca Miller, came up with the idea of *"tights for every skin tone."* As a matter of fact, based on her own experience and by observing markets, Bianca noticed that millions of dark coloured women suffered from not having tights that match the colour of their skin.[52] So, she wanted to address that shortcoming by providing tights for women with different tones of skins.

Therefore, market study can uncover pain points actually experienced by markets within existing trends. In the same line, if an idea does not address the pain points actually experienced by markets, market study will establish whether the improvement to an existing job to be done would be based on the subjective perception of the innovator. For example, if the Flowtab founders had interviewed markets, they would have known that queuing in bars to order drinks was not a pain point for markets. As such, they would have known that they would have had to promote the benefits of not queuing in bars to their markets.

Within growing and changing trends.
Next, within growing and changing trends, market study could identify whether markets would need to perform new jobs or whether they are starting to change the way that they address existing jobs. For example, in 1906, by observing markets, W.K Kellogg noticed that markets had started changing their breakfast habits from fat laden breakfasts to lighter grain ones.[53]

However, market research cannot predict whether the new habit or the change in habit would continue to grow. Market intelligence about the rate of change or the rate of growth of the respective trends would be a better indicator.

Creating new trends
Now, for ideas that create new trends, i.e new jobs that markets may want to get done, market research would not be useful in shedding light on potential market adoption. However, it would help determine whether the idea is addressing an existing job to be done or whether it is creating a job that markets may want to get done.

Often, innovators and entrepreneurs conflate *an existing job to be done* with a *job that markets may want to get done* and they use market research to gauge whether markets would be happy to adopt a new job to be done. Unfortunately however, the markets' answers would be unreliable. Case in point, Michal Bohanes asked potential customers if they would adopt the Dinnr idea. 70% of 250 respondents in the target market thought that it was a great idea.[54] However, as Bohanes admitted afterwards, it was a mistake. He thought that in reality what markets probably meant was that they were *"not entirely excluding the possibility that one day, when Ocado trucks run out of gas, supermarket doors get blocked by red-hot lava and restaurant waiters will, due to a mysterious leak of radioactive fumes emanating from commercial kitchen equipment, all be zombified and eat patrons' brains, yes, in that case they might be tempted to purchase a trial product. Once."*[55] Bohanes realised that it was a mistake to ask markets whether they would be happy to adopt the new job to be done created by Dinnr.

As it can be seen, just like the MVP, market research would also have different uses for different types of ideas.

Therefore, what could Dinnr have done differently?
Coming back to the case of Dinnr, the first question that Michal Bohanes should have sought to answer is the following:

How did the idea for Dinnr impact markets?
Was the introduction of variety in their everyday cooking, a job that young urban professionals were trying to get done or was it a job that they might have wanted to get done?

Therefore, the first step for Bohanes would have been to study markets to understand whether the introduction of variety in their everyday cooking was a job that they were trying to get done. Instead, he asked markets whether they would like the Dinnr idea and as he recounts on *Medium*, it was a mistake.[56]

As he recalls, he should instead have found out whether markets were tired of *"cooking bland repetitive recipes or ordering from takeaways."*[57] He also thought that he should have asked markets about the last time that they had tried to cook something new.[58]

In light of his account, [59] it can be inferred that markets were not seeking to introduce variety in their everyday cooking. Therefore, Dinnr had created a job that markets might have wanted to get done.

The next step for Bohanes would have been to identify the layers of uncertainties that his idea carried.

They were as follows:

Layers of Uncertainties For Dinnr

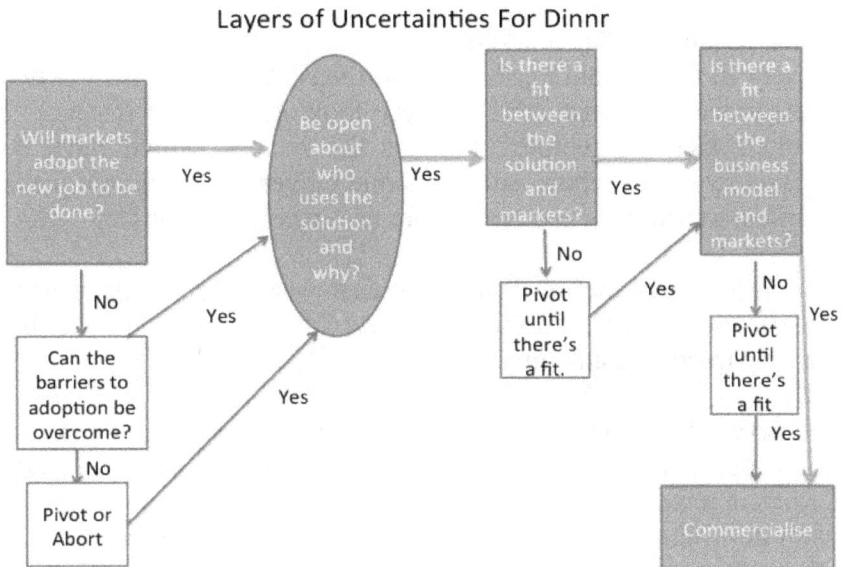

TOOLS TO ELIMINATE THE UNCERTAINTIES
MVP: Would have shown whether markets were ready to adopt the new job to be done. It would have also shown who interacted with the solution and why. The MVP would have ensured as well that there was a fit between the solution and markets and between the business model and markets.

Thus, the startup should have developed an MVP and tested the assumptions about the market's willingness to adopt the new job to be done. It should have also looked at who adopted the service and why. For instance, could such a service have suited retired couples who had time on their hands and who would have welcome the idea of introducing variety in their daily cooking?

The start-up should have also identified the barriers to adoption. Perhaps markets did not have the time to introduce variety or perhaps they preferred the convenience offered by ready-made food or takeaways? If that were the case, Dinnr could have pivoted or aborted its operations. An example of a pivot would have been to turn into a takeaway service. Another one would have been to provide recipes that could be cooked in a short amount of time – e.g 15 minutes.

Now, assuming that markets were open to the idea of introducing variety in their cooking, the question was: Was there a fit between the service and what markets were looking for? For instance, did markets like the recipes? Perhaps the recipes should have been created by known chefs, such as Jamie Oliver or Nigella. Or perhaps markets would have preferred more exotic combinations.

It may be worth noting that in the first week, the company had 12 orders and in the first 5 months, it had 220 customers, which shows that the trend was catching on.[60]

However, the company framed the idea as catering to an existing job to be done. Therefore, they expected adoption to be faster and 12 orders in a week paled in comparison with their projections. Perhaps with go-to-market strategies that were appropriate for trend-creating ideas, Dinnr would have gained more traction. Those possibilities will be examined in the next chapters.

Now, let's examine what Flowtab could have done differently.[61]

The layers of uncertainties for Flowtab were as follows:

Layers Of Uncertainties For Flowtab

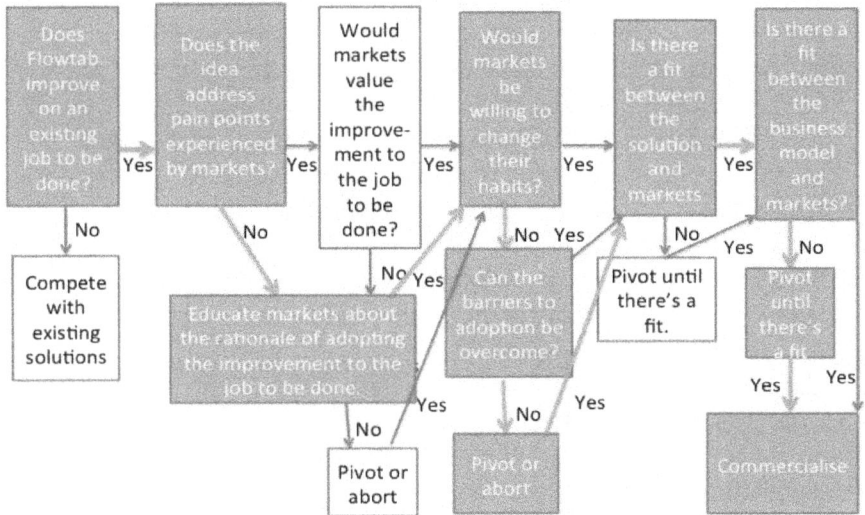

Flowchart: Does Flowtab improve on an existing job to be done? — No → Compete with existing solutions. Yes → Does the idea address pain points experienced by markets? — No → Educate markets about the rationale of adopting the improvement to the job to be done. Yes → Would markets value the improvement to the job to be done? — No → Educate markets about the rationale of adopting the improvement to the job to be done. Yes → Would markets be willing to change their habits? — No/Yes → Can the barriers to adoption be overcome? Yes → Is there a fit between the solution and markets. No → Pivot until there's a fit. Yes → Is there a fit between the business model and markets? No → Pivot until there's a fit. Yes → Commercialise. Educate markets → No → Pivot or abort. Can the barriers to adoption be overcome? → No → Pivot or abort.

TOOLS TO ELIMINATE THE UNCERTAINTIES

Market research/ study: Would have shown whether queuing in bars to order drinks, was a pain point experienced by markets.

MVP: The MVP would have shown whether markets would have adopted the improvement to the job to be done. It would have also shown whether markets were willing to change their habits and it would have identified the barriers to adoption. Finally, the MVP would have shown whether there was a fit between the solution and markets and between the business model and markets.

The idea for Flowtab was based on Mike Townsend's perception of how the existing jobs to be done of ordering and paying for drinks could be improved in bars. However, while the Flowtab team investigated bartenders' needs, they did not spend time with the other actors in the market, i.e bar customers. They assumed that their idea was addressing a pain point when in fact it was based on a subjective perception that markets wanted to improve on the jobs to be done of ordering and paying for drinks. As a result, they expected markets to simply adopt the solution and the idea failed.

Another important point to note is that Flowtab changed the habits of markets and the company never developed an MVP to try to identify whether the barriers to adoption could be overcome. If they had, they could either have pivoted or aborted their operations much earlier. They would have also identified whether there was a fit between their business model and markets. For instance, when they expanded to strip clubs, users were reluctant to order drinks on their smartphones because they preferred to remain anonymous.[62] Had Flowtab developed an MVP earlier, they would have identified those barriers much earlier. (See chapter 5 for full story)

The next chapter will now examine the different go-to-market and scaling strategies that different types of ideas would need.

(Note: The **templates** mapping out the different *layers of uncertainties* for different *types of ideas* can be found in the **Appendix.**)

GO-TO-MARKET AND SCALE

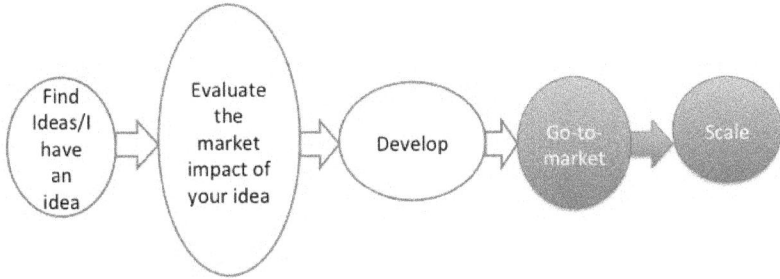

Find Ideas/I have an idea → Evaluate the market impact of your idea → Develop → Go-to-market → Scale

4. Go-to-market and Scale

Key Point:
1) Identify strategies for commercialising and scaling different types of ideas.

Dinnr created a job that the specific market of young urban professionals might have wanted to get done. Yet, the start-up did not really invest in advertising although the company was mentioned in several newspapers such as the Guardian, the Evening Standard and several other food blogs.[1]

In the same line, Rivet and Sway, the online eyewear retailer, relied on word of mouth advertising to change the habits of markets to buying eyewear online.[2] Unfortunately, the company could not survive and ended up closing its doors.

Question is: *What could the start-ups have done to increase market awareness?*

In order to answer this question, it would be important to understand how different ideas would require different go-to-market and scaling strategies and these will be examined on the following pages.

Adoption of new ideas would tend to vary based on the particularities of different industries. For instance, in the medical sector, commercialisation of new medical devices in Europe, must be CE marked, i.e they must conform to European directives regarding health and safety. Sometimes also, decision makers with regards to the purchase of new material will not be users. In other industries, adoption would be enabled only if an innovation is adopted by the industry leader. In still other industries, an innovation would be adopted only if it comes from a financially stable company. Therefore, it would be important to understand the mechanisms of adoption across industries, prior to the commercialisation of an innovation.

Yet, adoption would also vary based on how innovations would impact markets. Indeed, the Google, Salesforce, Amazon and Starbucks founders were aware of the market impact of their respective ideas and they adopted the relevant commercialisation and scaling strategies. For example, Marc Benioff from Salesforce.com knew that he needed to play the role of the revolutionary to change the habits of markets. Likewise, Jeff Bezos from Amazon knew that the company had to convince book buyers to shift their book purchasing habits by providing more value than the traditional way of purchasing books.

Those differences will be examined below.

A. Within existing trends

An interesting fact to note about Google is that back in 1998, the search engine's popularity grew essentially through word of mouth. This is not too surprising considering that a market for the idea was already present, i.e people were already using search engines and they were suffering from the inadequacy of the latter. Google's search engine addressed a pain point experienced by markets and it improved on the job to be done of internet search. Therefore, Google needed a form of advertising that could inform existing markets of the superior solution. As a matter of fact, *"in the spring of 1998, Brin and Page sent out an email newsletter to a list they called Google friends and urged people to spread the word."*[3] As expected, diffusion was rapid and scaling was proportional to the growth in market adoption.

In contrast, Rivet and Sway could not get away with word of mouth advertising alone. Indeed, Rivet and Sway was an online eyewear retailer that specialised in prescription eyeglasses for women. Just as Google's search engine, their idea catered to an *existing job to be done*. However, unlike Google, their idea entailed *a change in the habits of markets*. Thus, they had to inform and persuade markets to change their habits. However, cash poor, the company relied on word of mouth (just as Google) and online search, to drive consumer awareness.[4] As Sarah Bryar, the CEO acknowledged afterwards, in the post-mortem of the company, such a strategy made it hard to reach potential customers.[5] She also admitted that if she could do anything differently, she would invest much earlier in PR and advertising. As a result of the low customer conversion rate, they had to close down.

It can thus be seen that word of mouth advertising would not be sufficient for ideas that change the habits of markets within existing trends. As a matter of fact, the former CEO, John Lusk, knew that they had to *"drive awareness, educate women on why they should buy frames from Rivet and Sway, and try to change their current prescription buying behaviour."*[6] However, he also admitted that with limited budget, it was hard to do.

Consider now the strategy of Salesforce.com. Salesforce.com's SaaS impacted its market in the same way that Rivet and Sway impacted theirs, i.e it catered to an existing job to be done but it changed the habits of markets. However, unlike Rivet and Sway, Marc Benioff adopted a completely different strategy. The company had to inform and persuade markets to change their habits and therefore, Benioff *"embraced bold marketing tactics from the beginning in order to break through the industry noise."*[7] The first tactic was to hold a launch event at the San Francisco's Regency Theatre, which drew in more than fifteen hundred attendees. The event cost about $600000 but it *"earned them a firestorm of invaluable press."*[8] As part of its commercialisation efforts, the budding company hired a PR company right from the outset. It also *"educated the masses about the SaaS model and demonstrated that it worked."*[9]

Another interesting point to note is that at the launch party, Benioff *"played the role of the revolutionary because he needed to demonstrate that he was ready to lead the battle against the established software industry."*[10] Benioff led the change in habits from the use of enterprise software to software as an online service. Today, Salesforce.com owns around 22.3% of the CRM market ahead of the two enterprise software giants, SAP and Oracle, and it reports an annual revenue run rate of $6bn.[11]

Thus, if you have an idea that capitalises on an existing job to be done but that changes the habits of markets, just like Benioff, you would need to lead the change in habits. You would need massive advertising and PR to drive consumer awareness. You would also need to educate markets about the value of changing their habits.

As Salesforce.com's SaaS gained traction, Marc Benioff devised a strategy to take the company to the next level. As Benioff recalls, *"we needed to improve cash flow and to grow fast."*[12] Scaling ahead of the change in habits was especially important since the idea could not be patented and although Benioff did not want to act hastily, he was not willing to wait for long to grow Salesforce.com beyond its Silicon Valley roots. *"The need for CRM is universal, so I thought we could be successful everywhere."*[13] Since the idea was being widely adopted, and since the business model worked, Benioff thought that it would be only a matter of time before the rest of the world caught on with the change in trend to software as a service.

Now, consider how the iPod was commercialised. The iPod improved on an existing job to be done of listening to music on the go and it was invented as an answer to the perceived inadequacy of existing mp3 players at the time. However, as mentioned before, the improvement was based on the subjective perception of the innovators. As a result, Apple had to convince markets to adopt the improvement to the job to be done.

The *"iconic silhouette ad"*[14] was one means of reaching out to the masses. With the captivating message *"1000 songs in your pocket"*[15], Apple educated markets about the value of using the iPod. The company also created a hype around the iPod launch, seeking endorsement from celebrities in the music industry, such as U2 and Mick Jagger.[16] *"For a while, the company also offered limited editions of signed iPods by Madonna, Tony Hawk and Beck, and Oprah named it one of her favourite things."*[17] Apple created a buzz and generated enthusiasm around the iPod and it successfully led the adoption of its improved version of the mp3 player.

As a matter of fact, by the end of December 2001, three months after the iPod's launch, the company had sold 125000 units of the product. A month later, they launched in Europe. Then in 2002, they sold 600000 units and in 2003, they sold 2 million iPods.[18] Here, it can be noted that scaling was based on the reaction of markets to the product.

Scaling within existing trends
When it comes to scaling, innovators usually like to *"grow big fast."*

However, it would be important to look at how respective ideas are being adopted by markets, prior to scaling. Also, depending on how they would impact markets, different ideas would need different scaling strategies. For instance, Google's search engine addressed an existing job to be done of markets and solved a pain point experienced by a huge part of the market. Therefore, both adoption and scaling were quite rapid.

However, for ideas that are based on the innovator's subjective improvement to an existing job to be done, it would be important to gauge how markets would react to the improvement to the job to be done, before scaling is done. For example, Flowtab tried to scale before it had enough users, by partnering with Dex One (now Dex Media), their distribution partner, but the Flowtab founders were worried that their product and business model were not up to standard, when Dex One tried to scale too quickly.[19] And rightly so. As a matter of fact, markets were not willing to pay $1 per transaction by ordering for drinks through the app. Therefore, Flowtab should have fixed its business model before scaling.

For ideas that change the habits of markets within existing trends, scaling could be done ahead of the change in trend if there is proof that markets have started changing their habits beyond early adopters. The rationale is that it would be only a matter of time for markets to change their habits especially if the new solution markedly improves on existing jobs to be done. For example, Benioff thought that his company would eventually be able to convert other CRM users to SaaS.

Therefore, the factors to consider when scaling within existing trends would be as follows:

1) If the idea addresses PAIN POINTS experienced by markets, scaling would be relatively rapid.
2) If the idea is based on the subjective improvement to an existing job to be done, scaling should be done according to how markets would react to the improvement to the job to be done.
3) If the idea changes the habits of markets, scaling should be done if the idea has grown beyond early adopters. Early adopters are those who are happy to adopt anything new and so, it would be important

to watch how ideas are adopted by the rest of the market. Scaling should also be done if there is proof that both the idea and the business model are working.

B. Within growing and changing trends
Now, for ideas that capitalise on growing and changing trends, the commercialisation strategies would be slightly different.

As mentioned earlier, Netscape capitalised on the new job that needed to be done, i.e of internet browsing, due to the growing trend in the use of the internet. In order to commercialise the Netscape browser, Jim Clark, the Netscape founder, promoted the benefits of using the internet as well. Thus, *"he began travelling around the country extolling to various publishers what he believed were the growing opportunities offered by the web."*[20] The use of PR was also extensively used. As a matter of fact, Marc Andreessen, the inventor of the friendly browser, was portrayed as an interesting persona, probably to help lead the development of the trend. For instance, he appeared *"barefoot on the cover of Time Magazine."*[21] Since the growth in the use of the Netscape browser was directly proportional to the growth in the use of the internet, it was necessary to both drive the use of the internet and to inform markets of the available solution, i.e the Netscape browser.

For Amazon, the challenge was different. The company capitalised on a growing trend that was starting to change the way that an existing job was being done. i.e book purchasing. Therefore, the company first had to drive the growth in the use of the internet. Then it had to convince book buyers to shift to online purchasing. According to Bezos, the key was to *"offer incredibly strong value propositions to customers relative to the value of doing things in more traditional ways."*[22] Also heavy advertising was important to drive the change in habit, although in the early days, cash strapped Amazon relied almost exclusively on word of mouth advertising and public relations.[23] As a matter of fact, Bezos received much press coverage prior to the launch of the company. For instance, his door desk was mentioned in virtually every long interview and helped *"fuel the positive quirky press the company received."*[24] However, *"with the infusion of Kleiner capital in the spring of 1996, the company was able to think about spending a million dollars on an advertising programme. "*[25]

Similarly, Boo.com, the online fashion retailer that launched in the UK in 1998 and that closed down because it could not sustain its costs, invested heavily on advertising. Boo.com had good PR and it invested several million pounds on advertising. Yet, according to a poll by Mori, in spite of the company's heavy advertising budget, only 13.2% percent of internet users had heard of the company when the latter closed down and among non-users, that number fell to 1.4%.[26] Clearly not enough awareness had been generated. (See full analysis in chapter 5)

To summarise, if you have an idea that capitalises on a new job to be done due to a growing or changing trend, just as the Nescape founder, your commercialisation strategies would involve:
1) Driving the growth or change in trend.
2) Informing growing or changing markets of your solution.

If like Amazon's online retail website, your idea changes the habits of growing or changing markets, your commercialisation strategies would involve:
1) Driving the growth or change in trend.
2) Persuading markets to change their habits.
3) Informing markets of your solution.

Scaling within growing and changing trends
When it comes to scaling within growing and changing trends, caution would be advisable. Usually, if the idea cannot be patented, scaling ahead of the growth or change in trend would be preferable in order to ward off competitors. In that respect, Netscape did not have time to scale because it was beaten to the task by the software giant, Microsoft. However the idea of "internet browsing" continued to scale.

Jeff Bezos was equally fearful of competitors. As a matter of fact, he *"believed that Amazon.com had to grow as quickly as possible before the competition realised what was happening."*[27] There must however be evidence that the idea and the business model are working, as well as evidence of the growth in the trend. For instance, Boo.com, the online fashion retailer made the colossal mistake of scaling ahead of the development in the trend when internet penetration in the UK was only 20%.[28] The company should have had evidence of the growth in internet usage prior to scaling.

In sum, for ideas within growing and changing trends, scaling would require a careful assessment of:
1) How fast the trends are growing or changing.
2) Whether the idea can be patented or not.
3) Whether the idea and the business model are working.

C. Creating new trends

In a somewhat different vein, Starbucks created a new job that markets might have wanted to get done. As a result, they had to entice/lead the market into performing a new job. They had to inform and persuade markets to adopt the new trend. As Howard Schultz advises, *"in the building of a retail brand, you have to create awareness and attract people's favourable attention. You need opinion leaders who naturally endorse your product."*[29] Thus, *"Starbucks set out to educate their customers about the romance of coffee drinking."*[30] Also before they opened the first store, the LA Times named them the best coffee in America.[31] Starbucks also ensured that its employees became the enthusiastic and passionate champions of the brand. Employees' *"knowledge and fervour created a buzz among customers and inspired them to come back."*[32] Starbucks led the creation of the new trend, developed passionate champions of the brand and educated markets about the value of their service.

In contrast, Dinnr relied on word of mouth to develop market awareness. They were mentioned in few newspapers and online blogs. However, they did not lead the development in the trend. They did not educate markets about the rationale of adopting the Dinnr idea.

Thus, if you have an idea that creates a new job that markets may want to get done, just as Starbucks, you would need to lead the creation of the new trend. You would need to educate markets about the value of adopting the new job to be done and you would need to develop passionate champions of the idea. Lots of advertising and PR would also be needed to develop market awareness.

Scaling when creating new trends

The next challenge would be to scale the idea. For Starbucks, scaling was done ahead of the development in the trend, because Schultz was *"afraid of waking up the sleeping giants, the big packaging food companies."*[33] In what seemed like a scaling frenzy, Schultz planned to build 125 stores within five years.[34] The emphasis was also laid on *"offering the best coffee and customer service and an inviting atmosphere."*[35] Indeed, closeness to the growing market was maintained to ensure that the latter still favoured the company. Schultz wanted Starbucks to maintain its lead in the development of the new trend and so, he tried to establish Starbucks' presence in every city quite rapidly. There was however proof of adoption and every time that Starbucks entered a new market, they made sure that they developed local champions of the brand. For instance, *"they assembled a list of people who could serve as local ambassadors for Starbucks."*[36] They also tried to blend with the locals. As a matter of fact, in each market, they hired a local PR firm to help understand the culture and heritage of the place.[37] And they organised at least one community event in each market.[38]

To summarise, when creating new trends, scaling would involve an assessment of:

1) How the idea is being adopted. E.g. Is it being adopted by early adopters only or is there some evidence that it is being adopted by the rest of the market as well?

2) Whether the idea can be patented or not. If it cannot be patented, there would be a more urgent case for rapid scaling.

3) Whether the idea and the business model are working.

Coming back to the case of Dinnr, what could the start-up have done differently?

Considering that Dinnr created a job that the specific market of urban professionals might have wanted to get done, the start-up should have promoted the new job to be done to its target market. In order to do so, it should have promoted the concept of introducing variety in young couples' routines. For instance, it could have positioned the service as the answer to a romantic date night for young couples.

Dinnr should have also actively led the creation of the new trend and it should have sought endorsement from opinion leaders in its target market. Partnership with known chefs such as Jamie Oliver or UK Masterchef winners, could have promoted adoption. Lastly, the company should have sought lots of media coverage and it should have invested more in advertising.

As the company would have started gaining traction, Dinnr should have identified further barriers to adoption to ensure that there was a fit between its service and the growing market.

In the creation of a new trend, Dinnr should have adopted a more active commercialisation stance. It should have been at the forefront of the development of the trend, promoting the new job to be done, identifying the barriers to adoption and ensuring that there was a fit between the new job that budding markets were agreeing to get done and the solution that the company was offering. The fact that Dinnr wrongly framed the value of its idea, i.e, it thought that its idea was addressing an existing job that needed to be done rather than one that markets might have wanted to get done, was pivotal in Dinnr's failure.

In a similar vein, Rivet and Sway should have adopted different go-to-market strategies. The company capitalised on an existing job to be done of eyewear purchasing, but changed the habits of markets. Therefore, just as Salesforce.com, they should have actively led the change in habits that the idea entailed. They should have educated the market about the value of the change in habits. They should have also developed passionate champions of the brand and sought endorsement for their solution. And of course, lots of PR and advertising would have generated more awareness about the new solution.

The next chapter will further examine how other ideas failed because they were wrongly framed.

5. Explaining the failure of ideas.

Scroll through the 101 post-mortems of failed start-ups provided by CB insights and you would discover an astonishing fact: 42% of those start-ups failed because of a lack of fit with markets.[1] Even more cause for concern is the fact that the majority of those start-ups failed after raising capital. Likewise, other innovations such as the Segway and Webvan attracted lots of investment. However, they did not have the success that was anticipated by their respective founders.

Taking the concepts developed in this book, this chapter will seek to explain whether those start-ups could have done anything differently to avoid failure. It will examine failed ideas along the three axes of innovation and it will seek to determine whether failure could have been avoided by properly framing the market impact of ideas and by devising relevant development, go-to-market and scaling strategies.

Within existing trends

The Segway

To begin with, consider the Segway. The story of the Segway was broached briefly in Chapter 4 but this chapter will analyse the reasons why the Segway failed in light of the steps highlighted in the Innovator's Method.

The Segway is a two-wheeled electric vehicle that relies on a system of gyroscopes to remain upright. It was invented by Dean Kamen, with the purposes of replacing cars and of revolutionising travel within cities.

The value propositions of the Segway across the following market segments were as follows: [2]
Consumers: It was faster than walking and cheaper than cars
Businesses: It resulted in increased productivity, efficiency and employee satisfaction.
Universities: It was more convenient than bicycles around campuses.

Market Impact

Here, it would be worth noting that the Segway addressed the existing jobs to be done of its target markets. However:

1) Its value propositions were more based on Kamen's subjective perception of how the markets' respective jobs to be done could be improved, i.e Kamen never tried to find out whether markets were experiencing any pain points with regards to their existing solutions.

2) The Segway involved a change in habits.

Develop

Therefore, Kamen should have mapped out the layers of uncertainties that his idea carried. They were as follows:

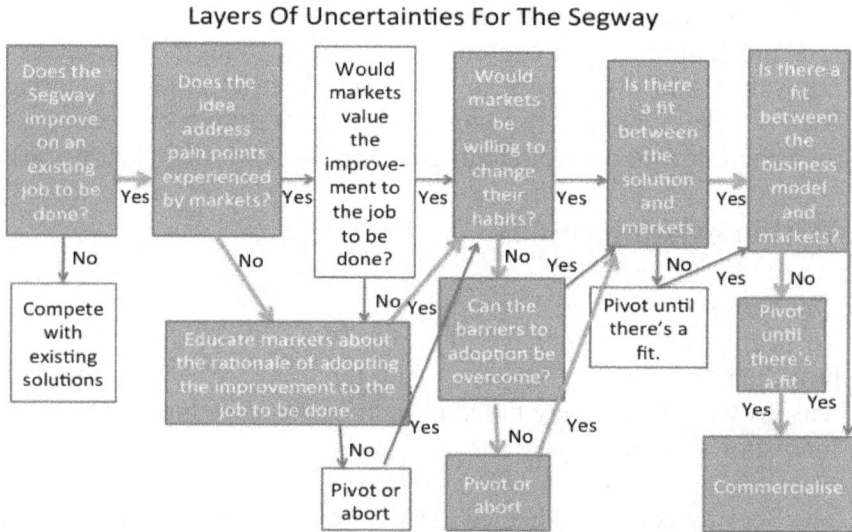

Layers Of Uncertainties For The Segway

In order to understand whether his idea solved any pain points or inadequacies experienced by markets or whether it was based on his subjective perception of how the jobs to be done of markets could be improved, Kamen should have studied markets.

Then, by launching an early prototype (an MVP), Kamen would have been able to address some of the uncertainties that the Segway carried. At that stage, he would have identified the barriers to adoption, e.g "*older employees' concern that they would fall over*"[3] or the inability of people to hold an umbrella on a rainy day while riding the Segway.[4] Co-creation with potential customers would have also ensured that the Segway was built around the need/ taste of users. For instance, people thought that the Segway made people look "*dorky*."[5]

Instead, the Segway was kept under heavy wraps until its commercialisation, and at a price of $4950, it was quite expensive.[6] Thus, during commercialisation, the company experienced what it should have experienced much earlier in the innovation process: its market's reaction, only much worse, because of the huge build-up in expectations caused by the media. Fit between markets and the Segway both in terms of product and business model was not achieved and the barriers to the market's change in habits were not addressed. As a result, the Segway did not have the massive market impact that it was expecting. According to the Time, from 2001 to the end of 2007, the company only sold 30,000 units of its two-wheeled scooter, which was a far cry from the anticipated result.[7] Indeed, Kamen predicted that by the end of 2002, the company would be selling 10000 units a week while his venture capitalist John Doerr thought that the Segway would achieve $1 billion in sales by the end of that same year, faster than any company in history."[8] However, adoption of the Segway was proportional to the rate at which markets were willing to change their habits and from a development perspective, unless the barriers to adoption had been addressed and the price had been adjusted to fit markets, adoption would have proven to be very slow, and it turned out to be the case.

Go-to-market
In terms of its commercialisation strategies, the Segway obtained lots of media attention prior to its launch. It was even endorsed by two prominent figures: Jeff Bezos and Steve Jobs. Yet, Kamen should have also led the change in habits, perhaps by playing the role of the revolutionary à la Benioff.[9] Since the improvement to the jobs to be done of markets was subjective rather than derived from market insights, Kamen should have educated markets about the value of using the Segway. Continued advertising, PR and leadership in changing the habits of markets would have been helpful in ensuring that markets changed their habits over time. However,

unless there was a fit between the product and markets, spending time and resources on advertising could have proven to be futile.

Flowtab

Let's now take a look at a different company that tried to improve on an existing job to be done but that was ultimately not successful. Flowtab aspired to streamline the drinks ordering and payment processes in bars by allowing users to order their drinks on their smartphones and the orders would be received at the bar on an iPad that was connected to the till. The value propositions were speed of service, no handling of credit cards, no queuing in bars and no handling of payments by bartenders.[10] Such a service resulted in an improvement to the jobs to be done of both bartenders and bar customers.

Market Impact

Yet, the improvement was based on the subjective perception of the Flowtab founders, on how the jobs to be done of ordering and paying for drinks could be improved, and it involved a change in the habits of markets. Therefore, the Flowtab founders should have mapped out their layers of uncertainties.

Develop

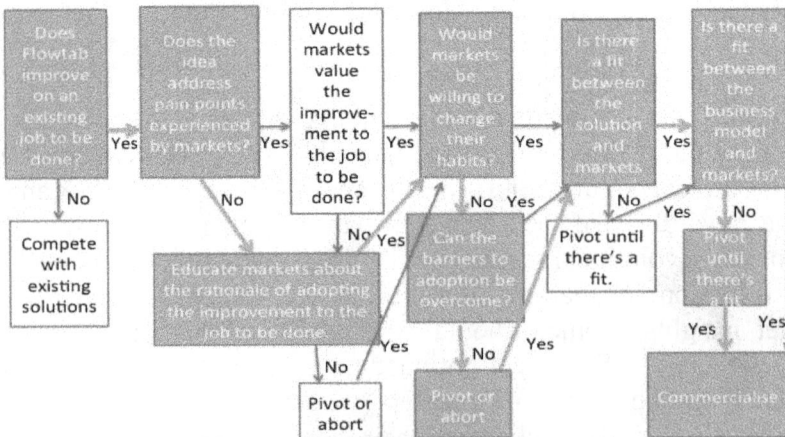

Layers Of Uncertainties For Flowtab

Prior to the launch of the service, the flowtab team *"hit the streets, talking to servers, bartenders and bar owners"*[11] in an effort to learn as much as possible about the industry. However, they did not meet with bar customers to try to understand whether Flowtab would provide significant added value. They did not involve bar customers at all in the development of their solution. As a result, they did not identify whether Flowtab would improve on the job to be done of bar customers and whether the latter would be happy to pay $1 per order. Here, it can be noted that the team should have conducted a more thorough market study.

The Flowtab team also did not identify the barriers to adoption. By releasing an MVP, the team would have noticed that poor network coverage in bars was one of the barriers to using the Flowtab app.[12] Also, when they tried to expand to a strip club, customers were not happy to use their phones to order drinks, as they wanted to maintain their anonymity.[13] By identifying the barriers to adoption early in the process, perhaps Flowtab could have come up with better alternatives or they could have aborted their operations earlier.

Go-to-market
In terms of commercialisation, the Flowtab team needed to persuade and educate markets about the value of using the Flowtab solution, because the solution:
1) Was based on the subjective perception of the innovators about how the existing jobs to be done of ordering and paying for drinks could be improved.
2) Changed the habits of markets.

The Flowtab founders also needed endorsement of their solution by influencers in their markets.

Thus, the Flowtab team organised a launch party at Copa d'Oro, which is a bar in Santa Monica, and they invited the mayor. The latter ordered a drink via the app. Although they had few technical issues, they managed to process over $1200 in transactions. Some articles were also written in the press about their event and the mayor's tweet contributed to the initial exposure that they needed.[14]

Their second major event was a pub crawl and although they

obtained 130 new users, their server crashed and it resulted in few 1 star reviews in the app store.[15] They also partnered with Dex One (now Dex Media), their distribution partner and were invited to be keynote speakers at the annual Dex One Conference in Las Vegas.[16]

Other events included the Niners Super Bowl party that they threw at Mayes Oyster House (a bar, restaurant and dance venue). They obtained 92 new users from the event.[17] However, after a year, they had only 12 regular users across 9 bars. *"We were spending about $7,000/month on marketing - mainly throwing events, hiring photographers and promo girls, organising meetup groups, posting in-bar signage, running social media campaigns and setting up affiliate programs with Lyft drivers and Flowtab bartenders. That generated high nightly orders (50-60) but did not generate much repeat usage. The adoption rate of Flowtab was much lower than expected, making the cost to acquire customers orders higher than any foreseeable revenue stream."*[18] They also struggled with poor cell reception and could not build a homogenous solution that would fit every bar.[19]

It would be however worthy to note that their *"launch events as well as the on-premise promo girls and their affiliate programs generated major spikes in user signups."*[20] Yet, although they ended up having 2000 registered accounts, they did not have regular users.

From a commercialisation standpoint, the Flowtab team did well to drive awareness and to lead the change in habits that the use of Flowtab entailed. However, unless there was a fit between the solution and markets both in terms of product and business model, spending resources on marketing and advertising would have proven to be futile.

Webvan
Another case that would be worth mentioning is Webvan.

Market Impact
Webvan was an online grocery retailer that was established in 1999 by Louis Borders. At the time, few grocers such as Peapod and HomeGrocer had already considered how the internet could improve

on the job to be done of shopping for grocery and they had launched their online grocery retail shops. In so doing, they had started changing the way that an existing job was being done, i.e grocery shopping. Louis Borders thought that he could do a better job than the nascent online retailers by offering an online experience that would surpass traditional retailing both in terms of costs and experience. Yet, by scaling too rapidly without addressing the uncertainties pertaining to the company's business model, the company had to close down in 2001. [21]

Develop

Thus, the first step for Louis Borders would have been to map out the layers of uncertainties for Webvan. They were as follows:

Layers Of Uncertainties For Webvan

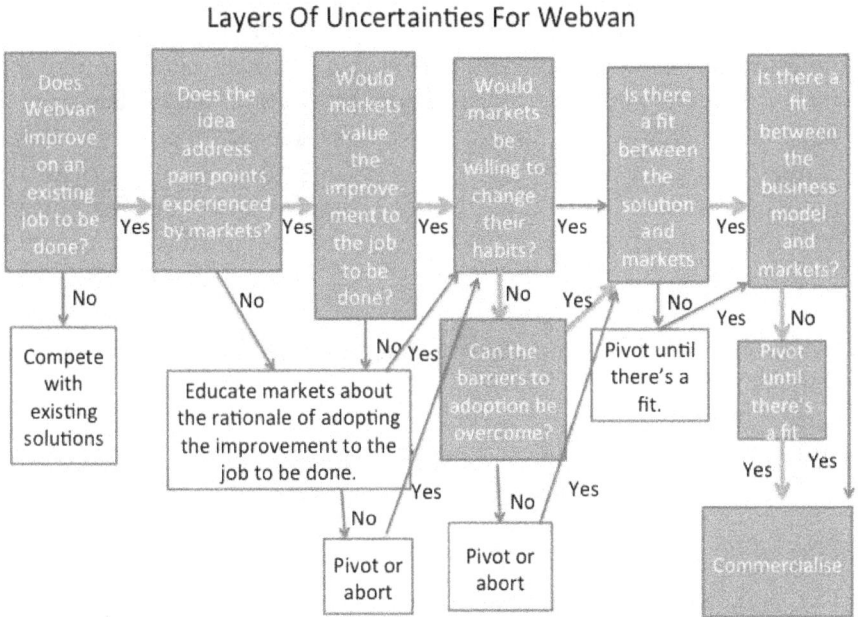

In order to eliminate those uncertainties, the company should have first studied markets to understand whether they were experiencing any pain points with respect to shopping in supermarkets and with existing online grocers.

Then, with an MVP, the company would have identified whether markets were ready to adopt the idea. The MVP would have also identified the barriers to adoption. For instance, the fact that delivery wasn't ordered the same day and that customers had to be at home when delivery was made, made it harder for markets to change their habits.[22] Also, the MVP would have identified whether there was a fit between the solution and markets and between the business model and markets.

Instead, the company scaled ahead of its operations when it was making losses in its primary market. By fixing the problem pertaining to the business model prior to commercialisation and scaling, perhaps Webvan could have avoided failure.

Go-to-market

In terms of its commercialisation strategy, Webvan knew that it had to focus on changing the mindset of markets.[23] The company invested massively on advertising. Since Webvan entailed a change in the habit of markets, Louis Borders should have also tried to personally lead the change in habits. He should have sought endorsements from influencers in Webvan's target market. However, unless there was a fit between the business model and markets, no amount of advertising would have solved the profitability issue of Webvan.

Next, let's consider how an idea that capitalised on a growing trend, failed.

Within growing and changing trends

Boo.Com

Boo.com was an online fashion company that was founded in 1998 by Ernst Malstom, a Swedish poetry critic and Kajsa Leander, a former Vogue model. Aspiring to be the *"premier online location where the cool and the chic would be able to buy their clothes,"*[24] Boo.com launched with 400 employees in eight offices.

However, in as much as only 20% of UK households had access to the internet, the company had few visitors to its sites and not enough sales to sustain itself. Furthermore, the website's features could not be fully accessed with the dial up connection in UK households.[25] As a result, the company had to close down two years later.

Question is: *Could Boo.com have done anything differently?*

Market Impact
To start with, Malstom and Leander capitalised on a growing trend in the use of the internet, to change the way that an existing job was being done, i.e fashion retail.

Develop
The layers of uncertainties that the idea carried were as follows:

Layers of Uncertainties For Boo.com

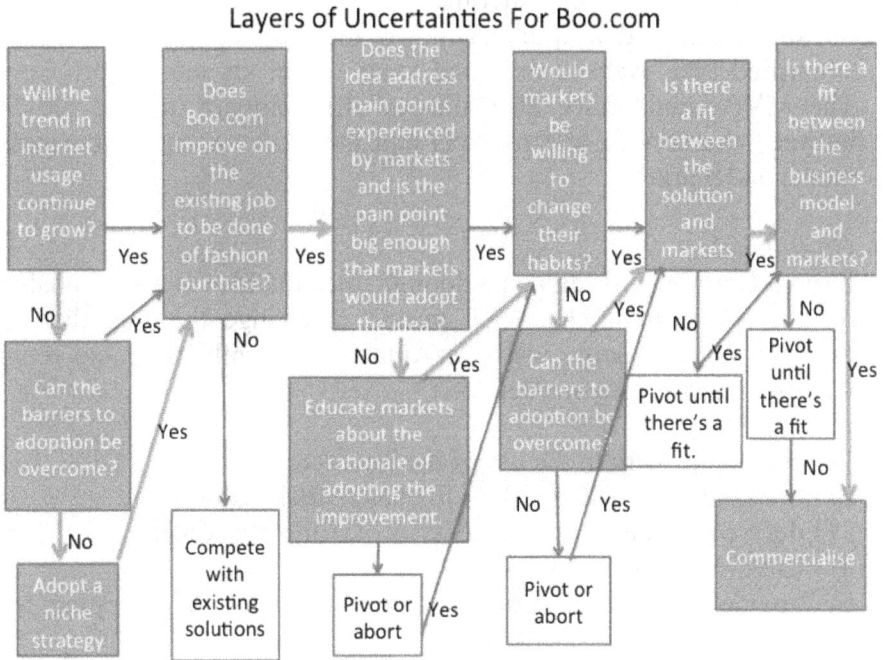

In order to iron out the uncertainties, Boo.com should have had market intelligence pertaining to the rate of growth in internet usage in its different markets. Market intelligence would have revealed that only 20% of UK households had access to the internet and that information would have enabled the founders to adequately gauge the scale of their initial business and potential rate of adoption.

Boo.com should have also conducted a market study to understand whether markets were experiencing any pain points with respect to the purchase of fashion. Then, the company should have ensured that Boo.com addressed those pain points. If the idea did not address any pain points, the start-up should have educated markets about the value of shopping online.

Then, with an MVP, Boo.com would have identified whether markets would have valued the improvement to their job to be done that the online service was addressing and whether they would have been willing to change their habits to buying online. An MVP would have also identified the barriers to adoption and it would have allowed the company to overcome those barriers. For instance, they would have discovered sooner that the features on their website were not supported by dial up connection[26] and they would have perhaps simplified their website or found ways to get around the problem. The MVP would have also allowed the company to test the fit between the service and markets and the fit between the business model and markets.

Go-to-market
From a commercialisation standpoint, since the idea was capitalising on a growing trend that was starting to change the way that an existing job was done, just like Amazon did with its online retail website, the company needed to:

1) Drive the growth in the use of the internet.
2) Inform and persuade markets to change their habits.
3) Educate markets about the benefits of using the service.
4) Lead the change in habits.
5) Provide more value than the traditional ways of shopping for fashion.
6) Invest heavily in PR and advertising.

In that respect, Boo.com had good PR and it invested several million pounds on advertising. Indeed, prior to its launch, the company was branded by Fortune Magazine, as one of the coolest companies in Europe. However, as mentioned before, a poll by Mori showed that in spite of the company's heavy advertising budget, only 13.2% percent of internet users had heard of the company when the latter closed down, and among non-users that number fell to 1.4%,[27] suggesting that the company should have perhaps invested more. However, unless the barriers to adoption had been overcome, an enhanced focus on advertising could have proven to be futile.

Now, let's move on to an idea that created a new job that markets might have wanted to get done.

Creating new trends

Plancast
Plancast was a social networking tool that allowed members in a network to share the events that they would attend. The team built a minimum viable product and launched it on Techcrunch. They initially had 100000 subscribers but after a year and a half, they could not expand beyond the early adopter community[28] and as a result, they had to close down. In the post-mortem of the company, the founder Mark Hendrickson established that the idea failed to scale because markets did not like to commit in advance to attending events.[29] There were also several other barriers such as geographical limitations and people liking to be invited to attend events rather than inviting themselves to events.[30]

The question is: *Could Plancast have done anything differently?*

Market Impact
To start with, Plancast's value proposition aimed at "*facilitating serendipitous get-togethers*"[31] by allowing friends to share the events that they would attend with members in their network.

The question is: *Were markets trying to have serendipitous encounters with their friends at events?*

Thus, the first step for Mark Hendrickson would have been to evaluate the market impact of his idea although based on the outcome of the idea, one can now infer that Plancast had created a job that markets might have wanted to get done.

Then, the next step would have been to map out the layers of uncertainties that the idea carried.

Develop
They were as follows:

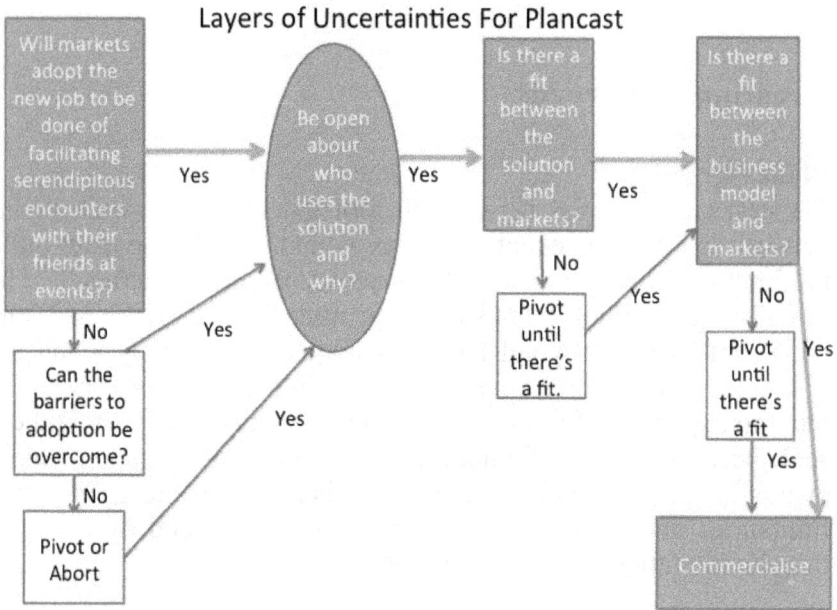

Layers of Uncertainties For Plancast

In order to overcome those uncertainties, Plancast developed an MVP and they *"were fooled into believing that the early traction validated the product."*[32] However, they soon found out that they could not scale beyond early adopters.

The new layers of uncertainties for the start-up were as follows:

Layers of Uncertainties For Plancast Beyond Early Adopters

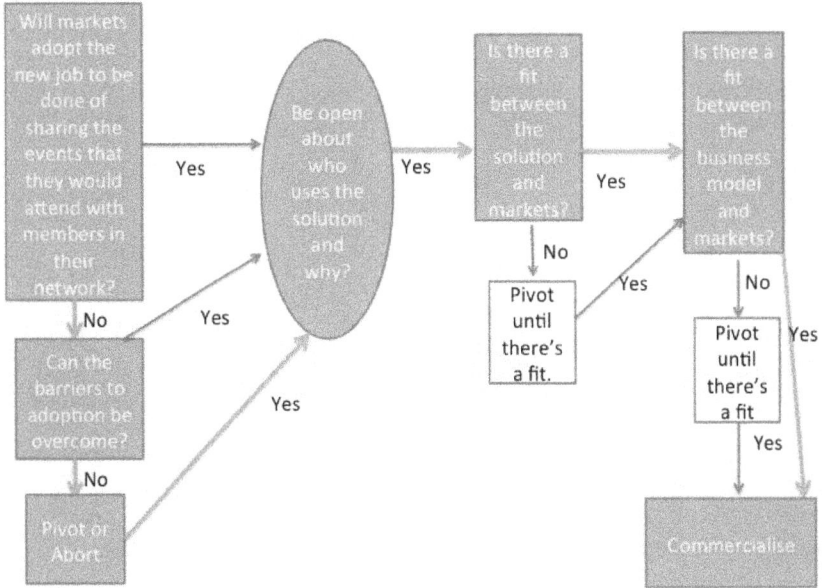

So, Plancast should have gone back to the drawing board and they should have identified the barriers to adoption. True, people did not like to commit in advance to attending events and some preferred being invited to events rather than inviting themselves.

However, could Plancast have done anything to overcome those barriers? For instance, could they perhaps have allowed members to uncheck themselves from events at the last minute? Or perhaps could they have targeted specific markets that like to share events for networking puposes? e.g entrepreneurs or professionals.

Go-to-market
With regards to the diffusion of the idea, Plancast launched on Techcrunch. It also participated in the major SXSW event.[33] SXSW stands for South by South West and is one of the biggest music and film festivals and conference that is held every year in Texas. However, Plancast was creating a new job to be done and so, the founders should have more actively led the creation of the new trend. They should have sought endorsement from opinion leaders and

developed champions of the idea. They should have educated the market about the advantages of sharing events. In fact, they should have more actively promoted the new job to be done to markets.

By overcoming the barriers to adoption and with a more active commercialisation stance, perhaps Plancast would have had more subscribers.

Conclusion

As an entrepreneur or innovator, you probably rely much on your gut feeling to evaluate whether your idea would be successful or not and your motto is probably to introduce your idea to markets as quickly as possible and to then see what happens.

Yet, take a look at ideas that were not successful and you would see that often, the entrepreneurs were as full of enthusiasm and of optimism as you probably are when you have a new idea.

Over the years, several books have been written to help innovators and entrepreneurs strategise more effectively to maximise the chances of success when bringing new ideas to market. Perhaps one of the most compelling books on the subject is the *Lean Start-Up*. The *Lean Start-Up* popularised the ground breaking concept of the *minimum viable product* (MVP)[1] which is a primitive version of a product that gauges the market's reactions as early as possible in the innovation process. The *"job to be done"*[2] concept broached in the *Innovator's Solution* has also helped entrepreneurs and innovators identify whether their ideas would be relevant to markets. Yet, in spite of those tools and strategies, some ideas still fail.

Taking a look at both successful innovations and unsuccessful ones, this book has uncovered an interesting fact; that different ideas would impact markets differently. More importantly, it has shown that based on their respective market impact, different ideas would need different development, go-to-market and scaling strategies.

In light of this, the Innovator's Method has been developed to help innovators and entrepreneurs successfully bring new ideas to market.

The Innovator's Method provides a framework for bringing new ideas to markets and it comprises of the following:

1) Find Ideas/ I have an idea.
Thus, **Chapter 1** has shown that innovation can happen along the following three axes:

1) Within existing trends.
2) Within growing and changing trends.
3) By creating new trends.

Within *existing trends*, markets would hire existing solutions to satisfy *existing jobs to be done*. Therefore, by understanding the existing jobs that markets would seek to satisfy, you could:

1) Identify how existing solutions would fall short of existing jobs to be done. For example, Google's search engine improved on the job to be done of internet search, especially when compared to existing search engines at the time.

2) Subjectively imagine how existing jobs to be done could be improved. For instance, if you wanted to improve on the job to be done of long distance communication, you could subjectively imagine how 3D holographic projection would provide a more real-life communication experience. Such an improvement would not be based on pain points experienced by markets. However, the latter could be open to the enhanced experience.

3) Identify how existing technologies or trends could improve on existing jobs to be done or could change the way that the latter are performed. For instance, the increasing use of smartphones is starting to change the way that markets pay for things. Mobile payment solutions are now available.

Next, *growing and changing trends* can create the need for new solutions by creating *new jobs to be done*. For example, Netscape capitalised on the new job to be done of internet browsing brought about by the internet. *Growing and changing trends* can also *change the way that existing jobs are done*. For example, Amazon's online retail website came into being when people started buying books via the internet. Therefore, you should monitor growing and changing trends and you should examine how those trends would impact markets.

The third axis along which innovation can happen is through the *creation of new trends*. The creation of new trends involves the creation of *new jobs that markets may want to get done* and they are usually harder to push to markets. Starbucks, for instance, successfully created a new job that markets might have wanted to get done, i.e enjoy the romance of espresso in a safe neighbourhood place.

As it has been shown in this book, those different types of ideas impacted their respective markets differently. Therefore, when you have an idea you should apply the second step of the Innovator's Method, i.e:

2) Evaluate the market impact of your idea.

Often, entrepreneurs and innovators come up with new ideas but they don't really know how their respective ideas would impact markets. Thus, as discussed in *Chapter 2*, by using market study, you could understand whether:

1) Your idea is improving on an existing job to be done.
2) Your idea is addressing pain points experienced by markets with respect to existing solutions.
3) Your idea is subjectively improving on the existing job to be done of markets.
4) Your idea changes the habits of markets.
5) Your idea is creating a new job that markets may want to get done. For example, if you have an idea that is not addressing an existing job to be done, it would mean that the idea is creating a new job that markets may want to get done. For instance, by interviewing markets, Dinnr would have understood that the introduction of variety through the use of recipes was not a job that the market of urban professionals was trying to get done, but rather, a job that it might have wanted to get done.

Within growing and changing trends, market study would help understand whether your idea addresses a new job that markets need to get done, or whether it addresses an existing job that is starting to be done in new ways. For example, by observing markets, W.K Kellogg realised that markets were shifting their breakfast habits from fat laden breakfasts to lighter grain ones.[3] A monitoring of how the respective trends are growing or changing would also be important to accurately gauge the rate at which your idea would potentially be adopted by markets.

Once you have evaluated the market impact of your idea, the next step would be to develop it. So, the third step of the Innovator's Method is:

3) Develop your idea

During the development stage, you would need to perform two steps:

1) Map out the layers of uncertainties that your idea would carry.
As it has been shown in *Chapter 3,* different ideas would carry different layers of uncertainties. You could thus use the templates provided in the Appendix to identify the layers of uncertainties that your idea would carry based on its market impact. For example, if as Salesforce.com's Software as a Service, your idea caters to an existing job to be done but changes the habits of markets, you could use *template 2.* If as the Netscape's browser, your idea caters to a new job to be done caused by a growing or changing trend you could use *template 3*. And so on.

Then, the second step that you would need to perform is:

2) Eliminate those uncertainties.
The tools to eliminate uncertainties have been described at length in Chapter 3 and they will briefly be re-examined here. They are:

A) Market Study/ Research
Within existing trends, market study would help you determine whether your idea improves on an existing job to be done. It would also help you gauge whether your idea addresses the pain points experienced by markets. Thus, by observing markets, Marc Benioff from Salesforce.com knew that enterprise software was cumbersome to users.[4] So, he devised a solution that eliminated that pain point.

Within growing and changing trends, market study would identify whether markets would need to perform new jobs. It would also show whether the growing or changing trends are starting to change the way that an existing job is done. For example, as mentioned earlier, by observing markets, W.K Kellogg could see that markets were changing their breakfast habits from fat laden ones to light grain ones.

Market intelligence would help you identify the rates at which the trends are growing or changing. For instance, Jeff Bezos knew that the internet was growing at the rate of 2300% per year and that books were the most sold items on the internet.[5]

Then, *when creating new trends*, market research would help determine whether your idea is creating a new job that markets may want to get done. Indeed, if your idea is not addressing an existing job to be done, it would mean that it is creating a job that markets may want to get done. For example, as mentioned earlier, by studying markets, Dinnr would have realised that markets were not regularly seeking to introduce variety in their cooking through the use of recipes.

Next, the second tool that is used to eliminate uncertainties is the minimum viable product.

B) A *minimum viable product (MVP)*

A minimum viable product would have different uses based on the market impact of ideas.

Within existing trends, it would help identify whether markets would be ready to adopt the improvement to their existing job to be done. It would also establish whether there is a fit between your solution and markets and between the business model and markets. For example, Google's beta test allowed it to test the fit between the search engine and markets. The beta test also showed that markets were ready to adopt the improvement to the job to be done of internet search. However, Google did not test the fit between the business model and markets, and for a long time, the company could not generate money until it came up with a viable business model.

For *ideas that change the habits of markets within existing trends,* the MVP would also show whether markets would be willing to change their habits and it would identify the barriers to adoption. For instance, the prototype for Salesforce.com's Software as a Service allowed the company to understand that no one was willing to be the first to take the huge risk of putting their proprietary data on Salesforce.com's server.[6] Thus, the company targeted pioneers who saw the internet as *"something new and exciting."*[7]

Next, within *growing and changing trends* that create new jobs to be done, an MVP would show whether there is a fit between your solution and markets and a fit between the business model and markets. And for ideas that capitalise *on existing jobs to be done but change the habits of markets*, an MVP would also identify the barriers to adoption. Thus, Amazon's beta test allowed it to understand that markets were concerned about putting their credit card details online.[8] So, the company came up with a secure system that was *"dubbed CC Motel."*[9]

Last, when *creating new trends*, an MVP would first of all show whether markets would be ready to adopt the new job to be done. For instance, by testing the espresso bar at the *"corner of fourth and spring,"*[10] Howard Schultz could find that markets were ready to adopt the romance of drinking espresso in a café. An MVP would also show who adopts the solution and why. And as in the previous two cases, it would also ensure that there is a fit between the solution and markets and a fit between the business model and markets.

Once ideas have successfully been developed, they would be commercialised. As it has been shown, different ideas would also need different go-to-market strategies.

Therefore, the fourth step of the Innovator's Method examines the different commercialisation strategies that those respective ideas would need.

4) Go-to-market

Within existing trends
As explained in **Chapter 4**, within existing trends, if your idea addresses pain points of markets, you would need a commercialisation strategy that would inform markets of your superior solution. For instance, Google used word of mouth advertising to inform markets of its superior search engine.

However, if your idea improves on an existing job to be done but if the improvement is based on your subjective perception, you would need to convince existing markets of the value of the improvement to the job to be done. Therefore, you would need persuasive go-to-market strategies such as: Lots of PR and advertising, seek endorsement from opinion leaders and lead the adoption of the improvement to the job to be done. Here, the commercialisation of the iPod was adduced as an example.[11]

Next, if your idea improves on *an existing job to be done but changes the habits of markets*, you would need to inform and persuade markets to change their habits. For example, Salesforce.com's SaaS strategy included the following: Educate markets about the value of the solution and about the value of changing their habits, lead the change in habits by playing the role of the *"revolutionary,"*[12] develop passionate champions of the idea, seek endorsement from opinion leaders and use lots of PR and advertising to generate awareness.

Within growing and changing trends

Now, if your idea capitalises on a new job to be done caused by *growing and changing trends*, you would need to both drive the growth or change in trend and to inform markets of your solution. In that respect, Netscape's founder travelled around the country to convince markets of the advantages of using the internet.[13] Diffusion would be expected to be proportional to the rate at which the trends are growing or changing respectively.

Next, if your idea capitalises on an existing job to be done that is starting to be done in new ways due to *a growing or changing trend*, your commercialisation strategies would involve: Driving the growth or change in trend and persuading markets to continue changing their habits. Therefore, you would need lots of PR and advertising. As a matter of fact, when Kleiner Perkins invested in Amazon, the company *"could think of spending a million on an advertising programme."*[14]

Create new trends

Last, if your idea creates a new *job that markets may want to get done*, your commercialisation strategy would involve convincing markets to adopt the new trend. Just as Howard Schultz did with Starbucks, this would involve: Educating markets about the value of your idea, actively leading the creation of the new trend, developing passionate champions of your idea, seeking endorsement from opinion leaders, and using lots of PR and advertising to generate awareness.

Once your idea has been successfully adopted, your next step would be to scale it.

This brings us to the last step in the Innovator's Method:

5) Scale your idea

Based on their respective market impact, different ideas would need different scaling strategies. Those strategies have been addressed in *Chapter 4* and they will be summarised below.

Within existing trends
To start with, when an idea capitalises on *an existing job to be done* and addresses the *pain points* experienced by a huge part of the market, diffusion would be expected to be rapid and scaling would be quite rapid as well assuming that there is a fit between the solution and markets and a fit between your business model and markets. In that respect, Google grew quite rapidly as the number of internet searches on their search engine increased exponentially.

Next, if your idea capitalises on *an existing job to be done,* but *changes the habits of markets,* you would need to consider whether:
1) Markets are changing their habits beyond early adopters.
2) There is a fit between your solution and markets.
3) There is a fit between your business model and markets.
4) Your idea can be patented or not. In the latter case, there would be a more urgent case for rapid scaling.

For instance, Marc Benioff, thought about scaling when the company was successful in changing the habits of markets in its home market. Benioff thought that it would be only a matter of time for the rest of CRM users in the world to change their habits.[15]

Now, if your idea *improves on an existing job to be done*, but if the *improvement is based on your subjective perception*, you could scale based on how markets would react to your idea, assuming of course that there is a fit between your solution and markets and a fit between your business model and markets. For instance, the iPod launched in Europe a month after its successful launch in the American market.[16] The reaction of the American market gave Apple the confidence to scale.

Within growing and changing trends
Next, if your idea capitalises on a *new job to be done* caused by growing and changing trends, your scaling strategies would depend on:
1) How fast the trends are growing or changing.
2) Whether there is a fit between your solution and markets and a fit between the business model and markets.
3) Whether your idea can be patented or not.

Here, it may be worth noting that Netscape could not scale because it was beaten to the task by the software giant, Microsoft. However, the idea of internet browsing grew rapidly under the aegis of Microsoft, as usage of the internet grew.

And if your idea capitalises on *an existing job that is starting to be done in new ways* due to a *growing or changing trend*, the additional criterion that you would need to consider is:
1) Whether your idea is being adopted beyond early adopters.
In that respect, Amazon made sure that the idea was successful with markets before it scaled.

Create new trends
Last, when you *create a new trend*, your scaling strategy would depend on whether:
1) Your idea is being adopted beyond early adopters.
2) Your idea can be patented or not. In the latter case, there would be a more urgent case for rapid scaling.

For example, once Schultz saw that the idea of enjoying the romance of espresso in espresso bars was successfully adopted by markets, he planned to scale quite rapidly before the competition was alerted.[17]

In contrast, Plancast, the social event sharing tool, could not scale beyond early adopters. [18]

As it can be seen, in as much as different ideas would impact markets differently, they would need different development, commercialisation and scaling strategies. By mapping out the layers of uncertainties that different ideas would carry, you could use the tools and strategies mentioned in this book to overcome those uncertainties. The different commercialisation and scaling strategies needed for different types of ideas have also been examined.

Hopefully, the case studies considered in this book, provide perspicuous and cogent illustrations that would guide you in your quest to successfully finding and bringing new ideas to markets.

Appendix

1. When innovating *within existing trends*, innovators would face the following uncertainties.

Template 1

Layers Of Uncertainties **For Ideas Within Existing Trends**

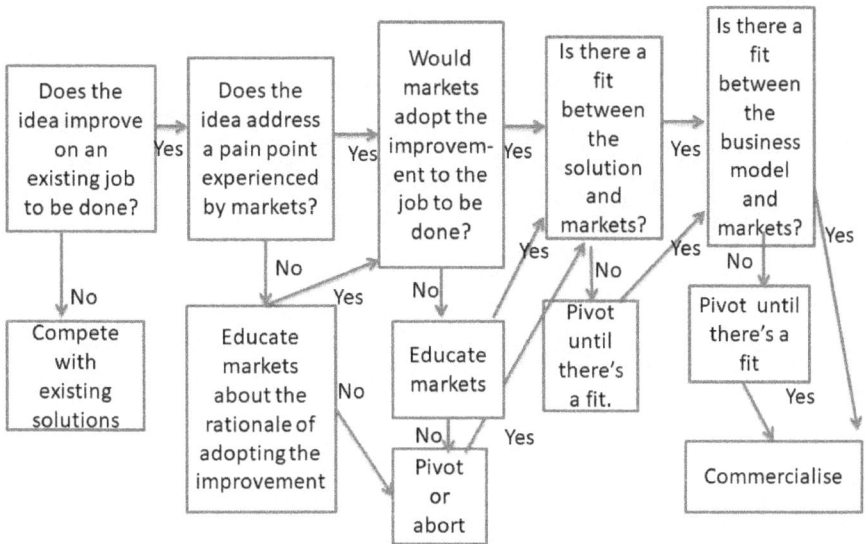

TOOLS TO ELIMINATE THOSE UNCERTAINTIES
Market study/ observation: Identifies whether the idea is improving on an existing job to be done and whether it addresses pain points experienced by markets with respect to existing solutions.

MVP: Identifies whether markets would adopt the improvement to the job to be done. It also identifies whether there is a fit between the solution and markets and whether there is a fit between the business model and markets.

For *habit changing ideas within existing trends*, innovators would face the following uncertainties.

Template 2

Layers Of Uncertainties **For Habit Changing Ideas Within Existing Trends**

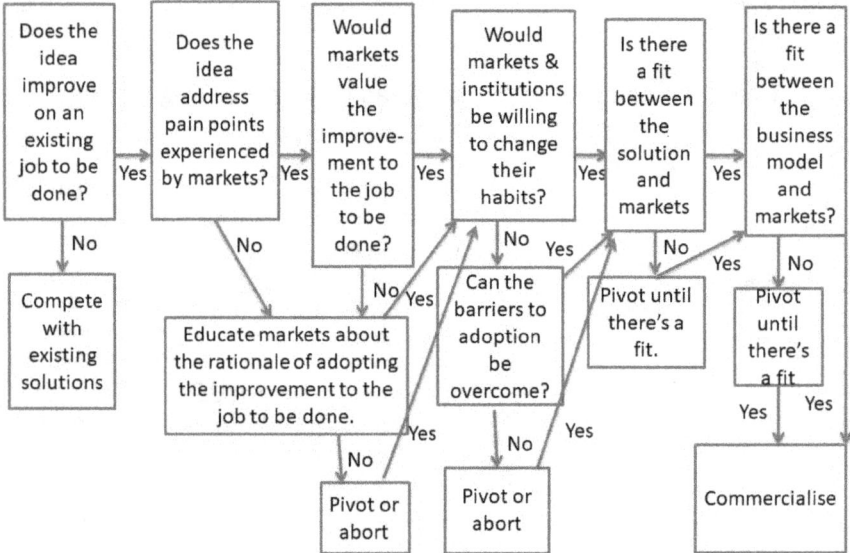

| Does the idea improve on an existing job to be done? | **Yes** | Does the idea address pain points experienced by markets? | **Yes** | Would markets value the improvement to the job to be done? | **Yes** | Would markets & institutions be willing to change their habits? | **Yes** | Is there a fit between the solution and markets | **Yes** | Is there a fit between the business model and markets? |

No → Compete with existing solutions

No → Educate markets about the rationale of adopting the improvement to the job to be done.

No / Yes → Can the barriers to adoption be overcome?

No Yes → Pivot until there's a fit.

No / Yes → Pivot until there's a fit

Yes → Commercialise

Yes / No → Pivot or abort

No / Yes → Pivot or abort

TOOLS TO ELIMINATE THOSE UNCERTAINTIES:
Market study/observation: Identifies whether the idea improves on an existing job to be done and whether it addresses pain points experienced by markets.

MVP identifies:
- Whether the pain point would be big enough that markets would adopt the idea.
- Whether markets would be willing to change their habits.
- Whether the barriers to adoption can be overcome.
- Whether there's a fit between the solution and markets and between the business model and markets.

2. Within *growing and changing trends*, innovators would face the following uncertainties.

For trends that create *new jobs to be done*, the layers of uncertainties would be as follows:

Template 3

Layers Of Uncertainties **For Ideas That Cater to New Jobs To Be Done Within Growing and Changing Trends**

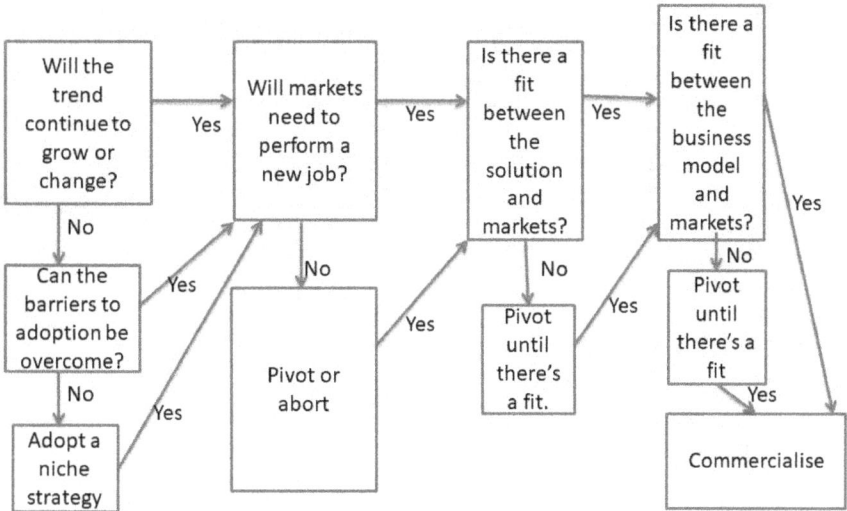

```
┌──────────────┐       ┌──────────────┐       ┌──────────────┐       ┌──────────────┐
│ Will the     │  Yes  │ Will markets │  Yes  │ Is there a   │  Yes  │ Is there a   │  Yes
│ trend        │──────▶│ need to      │──────▶│ fit between  │──────▶│ fit between  │─────▶
│ continue to  │       │ perform a    │       │ the solution │       │ the business │
│ grow or      │       │ new job?     │       │ and markets? │       │ model and    │
│ change?      │       │              │       │              │       │ markets?     │
└──────────────┘       └──────────────┘       └──────────────┘       └──────────────┘
     │ No                   │ No                    │ No                    │ No
┌──────────────┐       ┌──────────────┐       ┌──────────────┐       ┌──────────────┐
│ Can the      │  Yes  │              │  Yes  │ Pivot until  │  Yes  │ Pivot until  │
│ barriers to  │       │ Pivot or     │       │ there's a    │       │ there's a    │
│ adoption be  │       │ abort        │       │ fit.         │       │ fit          │
│ overcome?    │       │              │       │              │       │              │ Yes
└──────────────┘       └──────────────┘       └──────────────┘       └──────────────┘
     │ No     Yes                                                     ┌──────────────┐
┌──────────────┐                                                     │ Commercialise│
│ Adopt a      │                                                     └──────────────┘
│ niche        │
│ strategy     │
└──────────────┘
```

TOOLS TO ELIMINATE THOSE UNCERTAINTIES:
Market intelligence: Identifies the rate of growth or the rate of change of the respective trends.

Market study/ observation: Identifies the new job to be done.

MVP: Identifies whether there's a fit between the solution and markets and between the business model and markets.

And for *growing and changing trends* that *change the way that existing jobs are done*, the layers of uncertainties would be as follows:

Template 4

Layers of Uncertainties **For Ideas That Change The Way That Existing Jobs Are done Within Growing And Changing Trends**

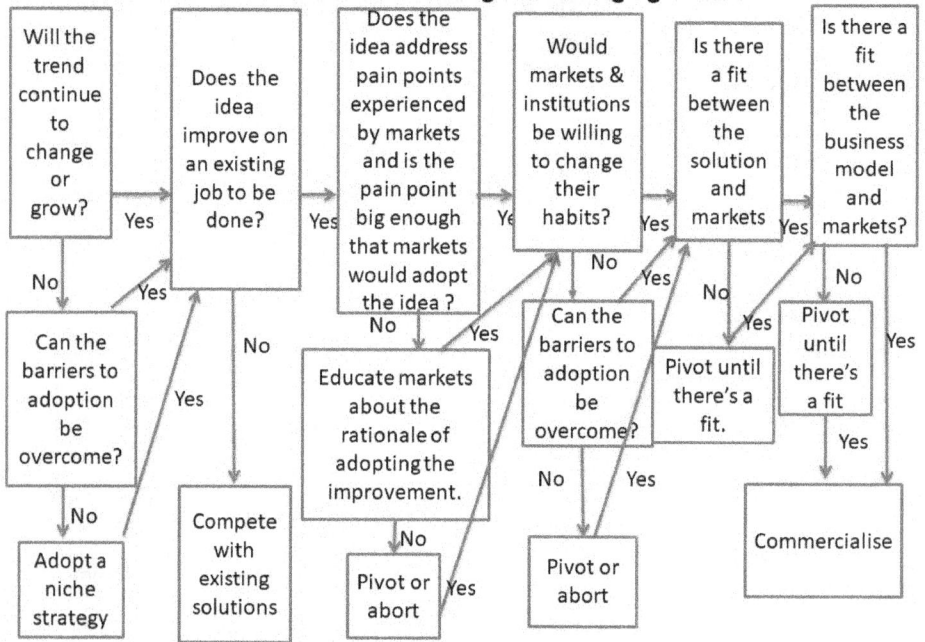

Will the trend continue to change or grow?	Does the idea improve on an existing job to be done?	Does the idea address pain points experienced by markets and is the pain point big enough that markets would adopt the idea ?	Would markets & institutions be willing to change their habits?	Is there a fit between the solution and markets	Is there a fit between the business model and markets?

— Yes → — Yes → — Yes → — Ye → — Yes → — Yes →

No / Yes

No (from habits) / Yes / No

Can the barriers to adoption be overcome? — Yes →

No — Educate markets about the rationale of adopting the improvement.

Can the barriers to adoption be overcome?

Pivot until there's a fit.

Pivot until there's a fit — Yes →

Yes

No → Adopt a niche strategy

Compete with existing solutions

No → Pivot or abort — Yes →

No / Yes

Pivot or abort

Commercialise

TOOLS TO ELIMINATE THOSE UNCERTAINTIES:
Market intelligence: Identifies the rate at which the trend is growing or changing.

Market study/observation: Identifies whether the idea improves on an existing job to be done and whether it addresses a pain point experienced by markets.

MVP identifies:
- Whether the pain points would be big enough that markets would be willing to adopt the idea.
- Whether markets would be willing to change their habits.

- Whether the barriers to adoption can be overcome.
- Whether there's a fit between the solution and markets.
- Whether there's a fit between the business model and markets.

3. Last, for ideas that *create new trends*, the layers of uncertainties would be as follows:

Template 5

Layers of Uncertainties **For Trend Creating Ideas**

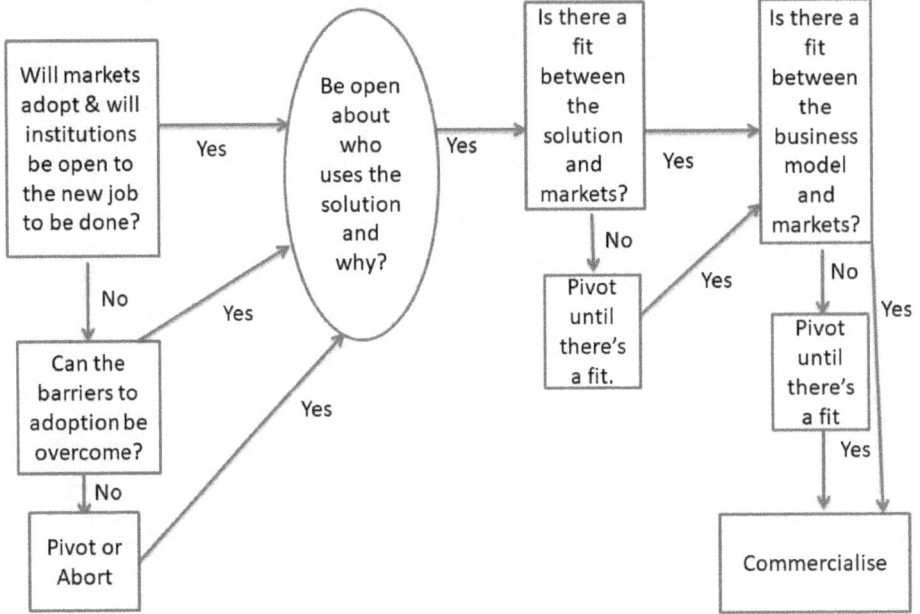

TOOLS TO ELIMINATE THOSE UNCERTAINTIES
MVP identifies:
- Whether markets would adopt the new job to be done.
- Who adopts the new job to be done and why.
- Whether there is a fit between the solution and markets.
- Whether there is a fit between the business model and markets.

About The Author

I am an Innovation Strategy Consultant and the founder of Next Curve Global, an innovation strategy consultancy based in London.

Throughout my career, I noticed that there was still a dearth of knowledge on the innovation process.

Therefore, my aim with this book was to bring some science into the process. By analysing both successful and unsuccessful ideas, I discovered a link between the market impact of an idea and its subsequent development, go-to-market and scaling strategies.

My background:
I have years of experience working as an Analyst and Consultant for a Strategy Consultancy.

I also hold an MSc in Innovation Management and Technology Policy from Birkbeck University of London.

If you have any queries or comments, please feel free to get in touch at: **melina@innovatorsmethod.com**.

With all my best wishes,

Melina Padayachy

Notes

Preface
1.CB Insights. (2014) *101 failure post-mortems.* (Online) Available at https://www.cbinsights.com/blog/startup-failure-post-mortem (11 June 2015)

Introduction
1.Cummings, E. (2013) *Word of mouth: Dinnr, an ingredients delivery service (Online)* Available at http://www.telegraph.co.uk/foodanddrink/10430663/Word-of-mouth-Dinnr-an-ingredients-delivery-service.html (11 June 2015)
2.Ibid
3.Wilhelm, A. (2013) *The decline and fall of Flowtab, a start-up story.* (Online) Available at http://techcrunch.com/2013/08/31/the-decline-and-fall-of-flowtab-a-startup-story/ (11 June 2015)
4.Bouman, J. (2012) *Flowtab brings express checkout to bars.* (Online) Available at http://techli.com/2012/07/flowtab-mobile-app/#. (11 June 2015)
5.Wilhelm, A. (2013) *The decline and fall of Flowtab, a start-up story.* (Online) Available **at** http://techcrunch.com/2013/08/31/the-decline-and-fall-of-flowtab-a-startup-story/ (11 June 2015)
6.CB Insights. (2014) *101 failure post-mortems.* (Online) Available at https://www.cbinsights.com/blog/startup-failure-post-mortem (11 June 2015)

Chapter 1.
1.Christensen, C & Raynor.E. M. (2003) *The Innovator's Solution,* Boston: Harvard Business School Press, 74
2.Christensen, C & Raynor.E. M. (2003) *The Innovator's Solution,* Boston: Harvard Business School Press, 76-77
3.Christensen, C & Raynor.E. M. (2003) *The Innovator's Solution,* Boston: Harvard Business School Press, 78
4.Schultz, H & Yang, D.J. (1997) *Pour your heart into it,* New York: Hyperion, 122

5.Vise, A.D & Malseed, M. (2005) *The Google Story*, London: Pan Macmillan, 35

6.Vise, A.D & Malseed, M. (2005) *The Google Story*, London: Pan Macmillan, 36

7.Vise, A.D & Malseed, M. (2005) *The Google Story*, London: Pan Macmillan, 36

8.Vise, A.D & Malseed, M. (2005) *The Google Story*, London: Pan Macmillan, 37

9.Vise, A.D & Malseed, M. (2005) *The Google Story*, London: Pan Macmillan, 4

10. Edwards, B. (2011) *The birth of the Ipod* (Online) Available at http://www.macworld.com/article/1163181/the_birth_of_the_ipod.ht ml (11June 2015)

11. Mixergy (2010) *LinkedIn's co-founder on why it took off- with Konstantin Guericke* (Online) Available at http://mixergy.com/interviews/konstantin-guericke-linkedin-interview/ (11 June 2015)

12.Benioff, M.(2009) *Behind the cloud*, San Franciso: Jossey Bass, 1

13.Benioff, M.(2009) *Behind the cloud*, San Franciso: Jossey Bass, 2

14.Benioff, M.(2009) *Behind the cloud*, San Franciso: Jossey Bass, 3

15.Chafkin, M. (2007*) How to kill a great idea.* (Online) Available at http://www.inc.com/magazine/20070601/features-how-to-kill-a-great-idea.html (30 Nov 2014)

16.Chafkin, M. (2007) *How to kill a great idea* (Online) Available at http://www.inc.com/magazine/20070601/features-how-to-kill-a-great-idea.html (30 Nov 2014)

17.Chafkin, M. (2007) *How to kill a great idea* (Online) Available at http://www.inc.com/magazine/20070601/features-how-to-kill-a-great-idea.html (30 Nov 2014)

18.Wilhelm, A. (2013) *The decline and fall of Flowtab, a start-up story.* (Online) Available at http://techcrunch.com/2013/08/31/the-decline-and-fall-of-flowtab-a-startup-story/ (11 June 2015)

19.Quittner, J & Slatalla, M. (1998) *Speeding the net: The inside story of Netscape and how it challenged Microsoft*, New York: Atlantic Monthly Press, 38

20.Ibid

21.Quittner, J & Slatalla, M. (1998) *Speeding the net: The inside story of Netscape and how it challenged Microsoft*, New York: Atlantic Monthly Press, 173

22.Spector, R. (2000) *Amazon: Get Big Fast*, London: Random House, 33

23.Spector, R. (2000) *Amazon: Get Big Fast*, London: Random House, 38

24.Ibid.

25.Spector, R. (2000) *Amazon: Get Big Fast*, London: Random House, 39

26.Ibid.

27.Spector, R. (2000) *Amazon: Get Big Fast*, London: Random House, 55

28.Spector, R. (2000) *Amazon: Get Big Fast*, London: Random House, 252

29.Benioff, M.(2009) *Behind the cloud*, San Franciso: Jossey Bass 122

30.Benioff, M.(2009) *Behind the cloud*, San Franciso: Jossey Bass 123

31.Kanaracus, C. (2012) *Gartner: Platform as a Service to see sharp growth* (Online) Available at http://www.pcworld.idg.com.au/article/442466/gartner_platform-as-a-service_market_see_sharp_growth/ (11 June 2015)

32.Kellogg history (Online) Available at http://www.kellogghistory.com/history.html (11 June 2015)

33.Kellogg history (Online) Available at http://www.kellogghistory.com/history.html (11 June 2015)

34.Wray, R. (2005) *Boo.com spent fast and died young but its legacy shaped internet retailing* (Online) Available at http://www.theguardian.com/technology/2005/may/16/media.business- Boo.com story (11 June 2015)

35.Ibid.

36.Williams, L.A. Biscuits move breakfast in new directions and vice versa (Online) Available at http://insights.ingredientsnetwork.com/biscuits-move-breakfast-in-new-directions-or-vice-versa/ (11 June 2015)

37.Ibid.

38.Schultz, H & Yang, D.J. (1997) *Pour your heart into it*, New York: Hyperion, 49

39.Schultz, H & Yang, D.J. (1997) *Pour your heart into it*, New York: Hyperion, 50

40.Schultz, H & Yang, D.J. (1997) *Pour your heart into it*, New York: Hyperion, 51

41.Schultz, H & Yang, D.J. (1997) *Pour your heart into it*, New York: Hyperion, 52
42.Ibid.
43.Ibid.
44.Schultz, H & Yang, D.J. (1997) *Pour your heart into it*, New York: Hyperion, 58
45.Schultz, H & Yang, D.J. (1997) *Pour your heart into it*, New York: Hyperion, 60
46.Ibid.
47.Schultz, H & Yang, D.J. (1997) *Pour your heart into it*, New York: Hyperion, 191
48.Schultz, H & Yang, D.J. (1997) *Pour your heart into it*, New York: Hyperion, 181
49.Benioff, M.(2009) *Behind the cloud*, San Franciso: Jossey Bass, 3
50.Lee Yohn, D. (2013) *What went wrong with Tata Motors* (Online) Available at http://deniseleeyohn.com/bites/what-went-wrong-with-tata-motors-nano (11 June 2015)
51.Ibid.
52.St John, W. *Barnes and Noble Epiphany* (Online) Available at http://archive.wired.com/wired/archive/ 7.06/ barnes_pr.html (11 June 2015)

Chapter 2
1.Bohanes, M. (2014) *Seven lessons I learned from my start-up Dinnr* (Online) Available at https://medium.com/@michalbohanes/seven-lessons-i-learned-from-the-failure-of-my-first-startup-dinnr-c166d1cfb8b8 (11June 2015)
2.Wilhelm, A (2013) *The decline and fall of Flowtab, a start-up story. (Online)* Available at http://techcrunch.com/2013/08/31/the-decline-and-fall-of-flowtab-a-startup-story/ (11 June 2015)
3.Danone history (Online) Available at http://www.danone.com/en/for-all/history/#timeline-1919 (11 June 2015)
4.Ecolab history (Online) Available at http://www.ecolab.com/~/media/Ecolab/Ecolab%20Site/Page%20Content/Documents/Our%20Company/Publications/MilestonesinEcolabHistory.pdf (11 June 2015)

5.Intuitive Da Vinci Surgical System (Online) Available at http://www.intuitivesurgical.com/products/davinci_surgical_system/ (11 June 2015)

6.Benedictus, L (2015) *Is this man responsible for inventing the selfie stick?* (Online) Available at http://www.theguardian.com/technology/shortcuts/2015/jan/11/meet-the-man-who-invented-the-selfie-stick (11 June 2015)

7.Stericycle history (Online) Available at https://www.stericycle.com/history (11 June 2015)

8.Forbes most innovative companies 2014 (Online) Available at http://www.forbes.com/innovative-companies/list/ (11 June 2015)

Chapter 3

1.Ries, E. (2011) *The lean start up*, London: Portfolio Penguin, 76.

2.Ries, E. (2011) *The lean start up*, London: Portfolio Penguin, 93

3.Vise, A.D & Malseed, M. (2005) *The Google Story*, London: Pan Macmillan, 39

4.Vise, A.D & Malseed, M. (2005) *The Google Story*, London: Pan Macmillan, 2

5.Vise, A.D & Malseed, M. (2005) *The Google Story*, London: Pan Macmillan, 4

6.Vise, A.D & Malseed, M. (2005) *The Google Story*, London: Pan Macmillan, 61

7.Vise, A.D & Malseed, M. (2005) *The Google Story*, London: Pan Macmillan, 84

8.Edwards, B. (2011) *The birth of the Ipod* (Online) Available at http://www.macworld.com/article/1163181/the_birth_of_the_ipod.html (11 June 2015)

9.Edwards, B. (2011) *The birth of the Ipod* (Online) Available at http://www.macworld.com/article/1163181/the_birth_of_the_ipod.html (11 June 2015)

10.Kahney, L. (2014) *An illustrated history of the ipod and its massive impact* (Online) Available at http://www.cultofmac.com/124565/an-illustrated-history-of-the-ipod-and-its-massive-impact-ipod-10th-anniversary/ (11 June 2015)

11.Costello, S. *Total number of Ipods sold all time* (Online) Available at http://ipod.about.com/od/glossary/qt/number-of-ipods-sold.htm (11 June 2015)

12.Benioff, M.(2009) *Behind the cloud*, San Franciso: Jossey Bass, 13)

13.Benioff, M.(2009) *Behind the cloud*, San Franciso: Jossey Bass,13

14.Benioff, M.(2009) *Behind the cloud*, San Franciso: Jossey Bass,13

15.Benioff, M.(2009) *Behind the cloud*, San Franciso: Jossey Bass, 69

16.Ibid.

17.Salesforce.com history (Online) Available at http://www.salesforce.com/company/ (20 November 2013)

18.Benioff, M.(2009) *Behind the cloud*, San Franciso: Jossey Bass, 70

19.Bhatti, J. (2012) CEO Interview: *Rivet and Sway wants to compete with Warby Parker by targeting women* (Online) Available at http://www.businessinsider.com/rivet-and-sway-wants-to-compete-with-warby-parker-by-targeting-women-2012-10?IR=T (11 June 2015)

20.Ibid.

21.Ibid.

22.Cook, J. (2014) The inside story of Rivet and Sway: Why this online retailer closed its doors (Online) Available at http://www.geekwire.com/2014/inside-story-rivet-sway-online-retailer-closed-doors/ (11 June 2015)

23.Ibid.

24.Heilemann, J. (2001) Reinventing the Wheel (Online) Available at http://content.time.com/time/business/article/0,8599,186660,00.html (11 June 2015)

25.Benioff, M.(2009) *Behind the cloud*, San Franciso: Jossey Bass, 120

26.Benioff, M.(2009) *Behind the cloud*, San Franciso: Jossey Bass, 123

27.Salesforce.com history (Online) Available at http://www.salesforce.com/company/ (20 November 2013)

28.Quittner, J & Slatalla, M. (1998) *Speeding the net: The inside story of Netscape and how it challenged Microsoft*, New York: Atlantic Monthly Press, 173

29.Quittner, J & Slatalla, M. (1998) *Speeding the net: The inside story of Netscape and how it challenged Microsoft*, New York: Atlantic Monthly Press, 203

30.Quittner, J & Slatalla, M. (1998) *Speeding the net: The inside story of Netscape and how it challenged Microsoft*, New York: Atlantic Monthly Press, 259

31.Quittner, J & Slatalla, M. (1998) *Speeding the net: The inside story of Netscape and how it challenged Microsoft*, New York: Atlantic Monthly Press, 69

32.Quittner, J & Slatalla, M. (1998) *Speeding the net: The inside story of Netscape and how it challenged Microsoft*, New York: Atlantic Monthly Press, 97

33.Quittner, J & Slatalla, M. (1998) *Speeding the net: The inside story of Netscape and how it challenged Microsoft*, New York: Atlantic Monthly Press, 53

34.Spector, R. (2000) *Amazon: Get Big Fast*, London: Random House, 33

35.Spector, R. (2000) *Amazon: Get Big Fast*, London: Random House, 65

36.Ibid.

37.Spector, R. (2000) *Amazon: Get Big Fast*, London: Random House, 168

38.Wray, R. (2005) *Boo.com spent fast and died young but its legacy shaped internet retailing* (Online) Available at http://www.theguardian.com/technology/2005/may/16/media.business- Boo.com story (11 June 2015)

39.Kellogg history (Online) Available at http://www.kellogghistory.com/history.html (11 June 2015)

40.Kellogg history (Online) Available at http://www.kellogghistory.com/history.html (11 June 2015)

41.Schultz, H & Yang, D.J. (1997) *Pour your heart into it*, New York: Hyperion, 86

42.Ibid.

43.Schultz, H & Yang, D.J. (1997) *Pour your heart into it*, New York: Hyperion, 86-87

44.Williams, L.A. Biscuits move breakfast in new directions and vice versa (Online) Available at http://insights.ingredientsnetwork.com/biscuits-move-breakfast-in-new-directions-or-vice-versa/ (11 June 2015)

45. Carnoy, D. (2014) *Amazon Echo Review* (Online) Available at http://www.cnet.com/uk/products/amazon-echo-review/2/ (11 June 2015)

46. Etherington, D. (2014) *Amazon Echo is a $199 connected speaker packing an always on siro style assistant* (Online) Available at http://techcrunch.com/2014/11/06/amazon-echo/ (11 June 2015)

47. *Introducing Amazon Echo* (Online) Available at https://www.youtube.com/watch?v=KkOCeAtKHIc

48. Fitzpatrick, A. (2014) *Your gadgets may soon be spying on your conversations* (Online) Available at: http://time.com/3576816/amazon-echo-microsoft-kinect/

49. Wray, R. (2005) *Boo.com spent fast and died young but its legacy shaped internet retailing* (Online) Available at http://www.theguardian.com/technology/2005/may/16/media.busine ss- Boo.com story (11 June 2015)

50. Spector, R. (2000) *Amazon: Get Big Fast*, London: Random House, 73

51. Spector, R. (2000) *Amazon: Get Big Fast*, London: Random House, 65

52. Miller, B (2014) *I lost the Apprentice but won't lose my dream of " nude" tights for all skin tones.* (Online) Available at http://www.theguardian.com/commentisfree/2014/dec/24/lost-the-apprentice-nude-tights-all-skin-tones (11 June 2015)

53. Kellogg history (Online) Available at http://www.kellogghistory.com/history.html (11 June 2015)

54. Bohanes, M. (2014) *Seven lessons I learned from my start-up Dinnr* (Online) Available at https://medium.com/@michalbohanes/seven-lessons-i-learned-from-the-failure-of-my-first-startup-dinnr-c166d1cfb8b8 (11June 2015)

55. Ibid

56. Ibid

57. Ibid

58. Ibid

59. Ibid

60. Ibid

61. Wilhelm, A (2013) *The decline and fall of Flowtab, a start-up story.* (Online) Available at http://techcrunch.com/2013/08/31/the-decline-and-fall-of-flowtab-a-startup-story/ **(11 June 2015)**

62. Ibid

Chapter 4

1.Linkedin. Michal Bohanes (Online) Available at
https://www.linkedin.com/in/mbohanes **(11** June 2015)
2.Cook, J. (2014) *The inside story of Rivet and Sway: Why this online retailer closed its doors* (Online) Available at
http://www.geekwire.com/2014/inside-story-rivet-sway-online-retailer-closed-doors/ (11 June 2015)
3.Vise, A.D & Malseed, M. (2005) *The Google Story*, London: Pan Macmillan, 43
4.Cook, J. (2014) *The inside story of Rivet and Sway: Why this online retailer closed its doors* (Online) Available at
http://www.geekwire.com/2014/inside-story-rivet-sway-online-retailer-closed-doors/ (11 June 2015)
5.Ibid.
6.Bhatti, J. (2012) CEO Interview: *Rivet and Sway wants to compete with Warby Parker by targeting women* (Online) Available at http://www.businessinsider.com/rivet-and-sway-wants-to-compete-with-warby-parker-by-targeting-women-2012-10?IR=T (11 June 2015)
7.Benioff, M.(2009) *Behind the cloud*, San Franciso: Jossey Bass, 26
8.Benioff, M.(2009) *Behind the cloud*, San Franciso: Jossey Bass, 26-17
9.Benioff, M.(2009) *Behind the cloud*, San Franciso: Jossey Bass, 86
10.Benioff, M.(2009) *Behind the cloud*, San Franciso: Jossey Bass, 27
11.Taylor, P. (2015) *Salesforce.com: Poster Child for Cloud 1.0* (Online) Available at
http://www.forbes.com/sites/sap/2015/06/08/salesforce-com-poster-child-for-cloud-1-0/ (11 June 2015)
12.Benioff, M.(2009) *Behind the cloud*, San Franciso: Jossey Bass, 86
13.Benioff, M.(2009) *Behind the cloud*, San Franciso: Jossey Bass, 169
14.Kahney, L. (2014) *An illustrated history of the Ipod and its massive impact* (Online) Available at
http://www.cultofmac.com/124565/an-illustrated-history-of-the-ipod-and-its-massive-impact-ipod-10th-anniversary/ (11 June 2015)
15.Ibid
16.Ibid
17.Ibid

18.Ibid

19.Wilhelm, A (2013) *The decline and fall of Flowtab, a start-up story.* (Online) Available at http://techcrunch.com/2013/08/31/the-decline-and-fall-of-flowtab-a-startup-story/ (11 June 2015)

20.Quittner, J & Slatalla, M. (1998) *Speeding the net: The inside story of Netscape and how it challenged Microsoft*, New York: Atlantic Monthly Press 123

21.Ibid

22.Spector, R. (2000) *Amazon: Get Big Fast*, London: Random House, 98

23.Spector, R. (2000) *Amazon: Get Big Fast*, London: Random House, 107

24.Spector, R. (2000) *Amazon: Get Big Fast*, London: Random House, 91

25.Spector, R. (2000) *Amazon: Get Big Fast*, London: Random House, 113

26.Wray, R. (2005) *Boo.com spent fast and died young but its legacy shaped internet retailing* (Online) Available at http://www.theguardian.com/technology/2005/may/16/media.business- Boo.com story (11 June 2015)

27.Spector, R. (2000) *Amazon: Get Big Fast*, London: Random House, 100

28.Wray, R. (2005) *Boo.com spent fast and died young but its legacy shaped internet retailing* (Online) Available at http://www.theguardian.com/technology/2005/may/16/media.business- Boo.com story (11 June 2015)

29.Schultz, H & Yang, D.J. (1997) *Pour your heart into it*, New York: Hyperion,116

30.Schultz, H & Yang, D.J. (1997) *Pour your heart into it*, New York: Hyperion, 246

31.Schultz, H & Yang, D.J. (1997) *Pour your heart into it*, New York: Hyperion, 116

32.Schultz, H & Yang, D.J. (1997) *Pour your heart into it*, New York: Hyperion, 245

33.Schultz, H & Yang, D.J. (1997) *Pour your heart into it*, New York: Hyperion, 114

34.Schultz, H & Yang, D.J. (1997) *Pour your heart into it*, New York: Hyperion, 105

35.Schultz, H & Yang, D.J. (1997) *Pour your heart into it*, New York: Hyperion, 115

36.Schultz, H & Yang, D.J. (1997) *Pour your heart into it*, New York: Hyperion, 255

37.Schultz, H & Yang, D.J. (1997) *Pour your heart into it*, New York: Hyperion, 254

38.Ibid

Chapter 5

1.CB Insights. (2014) 101 start-up failure post-mortems (Online) Available at https://www.cbinsights.com/blog/startup-failure-post-mortem/ (11 June 2015)

2.De Paz, R. et al (2004) *Segway: Crossing the Chasm*

3.Strategies Beyond Markets (2011) *Segway: How an innovation capable of changing the world fell in a chasm.* (Online) Available at https://strategiesbeyondmarkets.wordpress.com/2011/11/28/segway-how-an-innovation-capable-of-changing-the-world-fell-in-a-chasm/(11 June 2015)

4.Rivlin, G. (2011) *Segway's breakdown* (Online) Available at http://archive.wired.com/wired/archive/11.03/segway_pr.html (11 June 2015)

5.Masnick, M. (2009) *Why Segway failed to reshape the world: focused on invention rather than innovation* (Online) Available at https://www.techdirt.com/articles/20090730/1958335722.shtml (11 June 2015)

6.Devries, J.V (2010) *From hype to disaster: Segway's Timeline* (Online) Available at http://archive.wired.com/wired/archive/11.03/segway_pr.html (11 June 2015)

7.McIntyre, D.A (2009) *Failure to launch: Segway* (Online) Available at http://content.time.com/time/specials/packages/article/0,28804,1898610_1898625_1898641,00.html (11 June 2015)

8.Rivlin, G. (2011) *Segway's breakdown* (Online) Available at http://archive.wired.com/wired/archive/11.03/segway_pr.html (11 June 2015)

9. Benioff, M.(2009) *Behind the cloud*, San Franciso: Jossey Bass, 27

10.Wilhelm, A (2013) *The decline and fall of Flowtab, a start-up story.* (Online) Available at http://techcrunch.com/2013/08/31/the-decline-and-fall-of-flowtab-a-startup-story/ (11 June 2015)

11.Flowtab history (Online) Available at http://alpha.flowtab.com/ (20 December 2014)

12.Wilhelm, A (2013) *The decline and fall of Flowtab, a start-up story.* (Online) Available at http://techcrunch.com/2013/08/31/the-decline-and-fall-of-flowtab-a-startup-story/ (11 June 2015)

13.Ibid

14.Ibid

15.Ibid

16.Ibid

17.Ibid

18.Ibid

19.Ibid

20.Ibid

21.Peters, C, Okleshen, M. & D'Costa. *Webvan's Attempted Coup D'etat in the Grocery Industry* (Online) Available at http://www.learningace.com/doc/1201106/6a25dbc9750cf94e78152 d54ee0a5072/webvanforcls (11 June 2015)

22.Knowledge@Wharton. (2001) *Webvan finds that shopping for food online hasn't clicked with customers* (Online) Available at http://knowledge.wharton.upenn.edu/article/webvan-finds-that-shopping-for-food-online-hasnt-clicked-with-consumers/ (11 June 2015)

23.Peters, C, Okleshen, M. & D'Costa. *Webvan's Attempted Coup D'etat in the Grocery Industry* (Online) Available at http://www.learningace.com/doc/1201106/6a25dbc9750cf94e78152 d54ee0a5072/webvanforcls (11 June 2015)

24.Wray, R. (2005) *Boo.com spent fast and died young but its legacy shaped internet retailing* (Online) Available at http://www.theguardian.com/technology/2005/may/16/media.busine ss- Boo.com story (11 June 2015)

25.Ibid

26.Ibid

27.Ibid

28.Hendrickson, M. (2012) *The uphill battle of social event sharing: A post mortem for Plancast* (Online) Available at http://techcrunch.com/2012/01/22/post-mortem-for-plancast/ (11 June 2015)

29.Ibid

30.Ibid

31.Ibid

32.Ibid
33.Ibid
34.Ibid

Conclusion
1.Ries, E. (2011) *The lean start up*, London: Portfolio Penguin, 76.
2.Christensen, C & Raynor.E. M. (2003) *The Innovator's Solution*, Boston: Harvard Business School Press, 74
3.Kellogg history (Online) Available at http://www.kellogghistory.com/history.html (11 June 2015)
4.Benioff, M.(2009) *Behind the cloud*, San Franciso: Jossey Bass, xii
5.Spector, R. (2000) *Amazon: Get Big Fast*, London: Random House, 33
6.Benioff, M.(2009) *Behind the cloud*, San Franciso: Jossey Bass, 69
7.Ibid
8.Spector, R. (2000) *Amazon: Get Big Fast*, London: Random House, 65
9.Ibid
10.Schultz, H & Yang, D.J. (1997) *Pour your heart into it*, New York: Hyperion, 58
11.Kahney, L. (2014) *An illustrated history of the Ipod and its massive impact* (Online) Available at http://www.cultofmac.com/124565/an-illustrated-history-of-the-ipod-and-its-massive-impact-ipod-10th-anniversary/ (11 June 2015)
12.Benioff, M.(2009) *Behind the cloud*, San Franciso: Jossey Bass, 27
13.Quittner, J & Slatalla, M. (1998) *Speeding the net: The inside story of Netscape and how it challenged Microsoft*, New York: Atlantic Monthly Press 123
14.Spector, R. (2000) *Amazon: Get Big Fast*, London: Random House, 113
15.Benioff, M.(2009) *Behind the cloud*, San Franciso: Jossey Bass, 169
16.Kahney, L. (2014) *An illustrated history of the Ipod and its massive impact* (Online) Available at http://www.cultofmac.com/124565/an-illustrated-history-of-the-ipod-and-its-massive-impact-ipod-10th-anniversary/ (11 June 2015)
17.Schultz, H & Yang, D.J. (1997) *Pour your heart into it*, New York: Hyperion, 114

18.Hendrickson, M. (2012) *The uphill battle of social event sharing: A post mortem for Plancast* (Online) Available at http://techcrunch.com/2012/01/22/post-mortem-for-plancast/ (11 June 2015)

www.ingramcontent.com/pod-product-compliance
Lightning Source LLC
Chambersburg PA
CBHW070406200326
41518CB00011B/2090

* 9 780095 648242 6 *